C-1069   CAREER EXAMINATION SERIES

*This is your
PASSBOOK for...*

School Administrative Aide

*Test Preparation Study Guide
Questions & Answers*

COPYRIGHT NOTICE

This book is SOLELY intended for, is sold ONLY to, and its use is RESTRICTED to individual, bona fide applicants or candidates who qualify by virtue of having seriously filed applications for appropriate license, certificate, professional and/or promotional advancement, higher school matriculation, scholarship, or other legitimate requirements of education and/or governmental authorities.

This book is NOT intended for use, class instruction, tutoring, training, duplication, copying, reprinting, excerption, or adaptation, etc., by:

1) Other publishers
2) Proprietors and/or Instructors of "Coaching" and/or Preparatory Courses
3) Personnel and/or Training Divisions of commercial, industrial, and governmental organizations
4) Schools, colleges, or universities and/or their departments and staffs, including teachers and other personnel
5) Testing Agencies or Bureaus
6) Study groups which seek by the purchase of a single volume to copy and/or duplicate and/or adapt this material for use by the group as a whole without having purchased individual volumes for each of the members of the group
7) Et al.

Such persons would be in violation of appropriate Federal and State statutes.

PROVISION OF LICENSING AGREEMENTS – Recognized educational, commercial, industrial, and governmental institutions and organizations, and others legitimately engaged in educational pursuits, including training, testing, and measurement activities, may address request for a licensing agreement to the copyright owners, who will determine whether, and under what conditions, including fees and charges, the materials in this book may be used them. In other words, a licensing facility exists for the legitimate use of the material in this book on other than an individual basis. However, it is asseverated and affirmed here that the material in this book CANNOT be used without the receipt of the express permission of such a licensing agreement from the Publishers. Inquiries re licensing should be addressed to the company, attention rights and permissions department.

All rights reserved, including the right of reproduction in whole or in part, in any form or by any means, electronic or mechanical, including photocopying, recording, or by any information storage and retrieval system, without permission in writing from the Publisher.

Copyright © 2024 by
National Learning Corporation

212 Michael Drive, Syosset, NY 11791
(516) 921-8888 • www.passbooks.com
E-mail: info@passbooks.com

PUBLISHED IN THE UNITED STATES OF AMERICA

PASSBOOK® SERIES

THE *PASSBOOK® SERIES* has been created to prepare applicants and candidates for the ultimate academic battlefield – the examination room.

At some time in our lives, each and every one of us may be required to take an examination – for validation, matriculation, admission, qualification, registration, certification, or licensure.

Based on the assumption that every applicant or candidate has met the basic formal educational standards, has taken the required number of courses, and read the necessary texts, the *PASSBOOK® SERIES* furnishes the one special preparation which may assure passing with confidence, instead of failing with insecurity. Examination questions – together with answers – are furnished as the basic vehicle for study so that the mysteries of the examination and its compounding difficulties may be eliminated or diminished by a sure method.

This book is meant to help you pass your examination provided that you qualify and are serious in your objective.

The entire field is reviewed through the huge store of content information which is succinctly presented through a provocative and challenging approach – the question-and-answer method.

A climate of success is established by furnishing the correct answers at the end of each test.

You soon learn to recognize types of questions, forms of questions, and patterns of questioning. You may even begin to anticipate expected outcomes.

You perceive that many questions are repeated or adapted so that you can gain acute insights, which may enable you to score many sure points.

You learn how to confront new questions, or types of questions, and to attack them confidently and work out the correct answers.

You note objectives and emphases, and recognize pitfalls and dangers, so that you may make positive educational adjustments.

Moreover, you are kept fully informed in relation to new concepts, methods, practices, and directions in the field.

You discover that you are actually taking the examination all the time: you are preparing for the examination by "taking" an examination, not by reading extraneous and/or supererogatory textbooks.

In short, this PASSBOOK®, used directedly, should be an important factor in helping you to pass your test.

SCHOOL ADMINISTRATIVE AIDE

DUTIES
Performs routine duties of quasi-administrative nature as an adjunct to administration. Counts, marks, codes and distributes all textbooks; takes inventory at year's end. Requisitions and routes audio-visual equipment and material. Arranges assembly programs, provides props and facilities, and schedules activities. Calls substitutes, makes out time sheets and distributes checks. Receives complaints and refers them to the proper parties. Does related work as required.

SCOPE OF THE EXAMINATION
The written test will cover knowledge, skills and/or abilities in such areas as:

1. Coding/decoding information;
2. Name and number checking;
3. Office record keeping; and
4. Understanding and interpreting written material.

HOW TO TAKE A TEST

I. YOU MUST PASS AN EXAMINATION

A. *WHAT EVERY CANDIDATE SHOULD KNOW*

Examination applicants often ask us for help in preparing for the written test. What can I study in advance? What kinds of questions will be asked? How will the test be given? How will the papers be graded?

As an applicant for a civil service examination, you may be wondering about some of these things. Our purpose here is to suggest effective methods of advance study and to describe civil service examinations.

Your chances for success on this examination can be increased if you know how to prepare. Those "pre-examination jitters" can be reduced if you know what to expect. You can even experience an adventure in good citizenship if you know why civil service exams are given.

B. *WHY ARE CIVIL SERVICE EXAMINATIONS GIVEN?*

Civil service examinations are important to you in two ways. As a citizen, you want public jobs filled by employees who know how to do their work. As a job seeker, you want a fair chance to compete for that job on an equal footing with other candidates. The best-known means of accomplishing this two-fold goal is the competitive examination.

Exams are widely publicized throughout the nation. They may be administered for jobs in federal, state, city, municipal, town or village governments or agencies.

Any citizen may apply, with some limitations, such as the age or residence of applicants. Your experience and education may be reviewed to see whether you meet the requirements for the particular examination. When these requirements exist, they are reasonable and applied consistently to all applicants. Thus, a competitive examination may cause you some uneasiness now, but it is your privilege and safeguard.

C. *HOW ARE CIVIL SERVICE EXAMS DEVELOPED?*

Examinations are carefully written by trained technicians who are specialists in the field known as "psychological measurement," in consultation with recognized authorities in the field of work that the test will cover. These experts recommend the subject matter areas or skills to be tested; only those knowledges or skills important to your success on the job are included. The most reliable books and source materials available are used as references. Together, the experts and technicians judge the difficulty level of the questions.

Test technicians know how to phrase questions so that the problem is clearly stated. Their ethics do not permit "trick" or "catch" questions. Questions may have been tried out on sample groups, or subjected to statistical analysis, to determine their usefulness.

Written tests are often used in combination with performance tests, ratings of training and experience, and oral interviews. All of these measures combine to form the best-known means of finding the right person for the right job.

II. HOW TO PASS THE WRITTEN TEST

A. NATURE OF THE EXAMINATION

To prepare intelligently for civil service examinations, you should know how they differ from school examinations you have taken. In school you were assigned certain definite pages to read or subjects to cover. The examination questions were quite detailed and usually emphasized memory. Civil service exams, on the other hand, try to discover your present ability to perform the duties of a position, plus your potentiality to learn these duties. In other words, a civil service exam attempts to predict how successful you will be. Questions cover such a broad area that they cannot be as minute and detailed as school exam questions.

In the public service similar kinds of work, or positions, are grouped together in one "class." This process is known as *position-classification*. All the positions in a class are paid according to the salary range for that class. One class title covers all of these positions, and they are all tested by the same examination.

B. FOUR BASIC STEPS

1) Study the announcement

How, then, can you know what subjects to study? Our best answer is: "Learn as much as possible about the class of positions for which you've applied." The exam will test the knowledge, skills and abilities needed to do the work.

Your most valuable source of information about the position you want is the official exam announcement. This announcement lists the training and experience qualifications. Check these standards and apply only if you come reasonably close to meeting them.

The brief description of the position in the examination announcement offers some clues to the subjects which will be tested. Think about the job itself. Review the duties in your mind. Can you perform them, or are there some in which you are rusty? Fill in the blank spots in your preparation.

Many jurisdictions preview the written test in the exam announcement by including a section called "Knowledge and Abilities Required," "Scope of the Examination," or some similar heading. Here you will find out specifically what fields will be tested.

2) Review your own background

Once you learn in general what the position is all about, and what you need to know to do the work, ask yourself which subjects you already know fairly well and which need improvement. You may wonder whether to concentrate on improving your strong areas or on building some background in your fields of weakness. When the announcement has specified "some knowledge" or "considerable knowledge," or has used adjectives like "beginning principles of…" or "advanced … methods," you can get a clue as to the number and difficulty of questions to be asked in any given field. More questions, and hence broader coverage, would be included for those subjects which are more important in the work. Now weigh your strengths and weaknesses against the job requirements and prepare accordingly.

3) Determine the level of the position

Another way to tell how intensively you should prepare is to understand the level of the job for which you are applying. Is it the entering level? In other words, is this the position in which beginners in a field of work are hired? Or is it an intermediate or advanced level? Sometimes this is indicated by such words as "Junior" or "Senior" in the class title. Other jurisdictions use Roman numerals to designate the level – Clerk I, Clerk II, for example. The word "Supervisor" sometimes appears in the title. If the level is not indicated by the title, check the description of duties. Will you be working under very close supervision, or will you have responsibility for independent decisions in this work?

4) Choose appropriate study materials

Now that you know the subjects to be examined and the relative amount of each subject to be covered, you can choose suitable study materials. For beginning level jobs, or even advanced ones, if you have a pronounced weakness in some aspect of your training, read a modern, standard textbook in that field. Be sure it is up to date and has general coverage. Such books are normally available at your library, and the librarian will be glad to help you locate one. For entry-level positions, questions of appropriate difficulty are chosen – neither highly advanced questions, nor those too simple. Such questions require careful thought but not advanced training.

If the position for which you are applying is technical or advanced, you will read more advanced, specialized material. If you are already familiar with the basic principles of your field, elementary textbooks would waste your time. Concentrate on advanced textbooks and technical periodicals. Think through the concepts and review difficult problems in your field.

These are all general sources. You can get more ideas on your own initiative, following these leads. For example, training manuals and publications of the government agency which employs workers in your field can be useful, particularly for technical and professional positions. A letter or visit to the government department involved may result in more specific study suggestions, and certainly will provide you with a more definite idea of the exact nature of the position you are seeking.

III. KINDS OF TESTS

Tests are used for purposes other than measuring knowledge and ability to perform specified duties. For some positions, it is equally important to test ability to make adjustments to new situations or to profit from training. In others, basic mental abilities not dependent on information are essential. Questions which test these things may not appear as pertinent to the duties of the position as those which test for knowledge and information. Yet they are often highly important parts of a fair examination. For very general questions, it is almost impossible to help you direct your study efforts. What we can do is to point out some of the more common of these general abilities needed in public service positions and describe some typical questions.

1) General information

Broad, general information has been found useful for predicting job success in some kinds of work. This is tested in a variety of ways, from vocabulary lists to questions about current events. Basic background in some field of work, such as sociology or economics, may be sampled in a group of questions. Often these are principles which have become familiar to most persons through exposure rather than through formal training. It is difficult to advise you how to study for these questions; being alert to the world around you is our best suggestion.

2) Verbal ability

An example of an ability needed in many positions is verbal or language ability. Verbal ability is, in brief, the ability to use and understand words. Vocabulary and grammar tests are typical measures of this ability. Reading comprehension or paragraph interpretation questions are common in many kinds of civil service tests. You are given a paragraph of written material and asked to find its central meaning.

3) Numerical ability

Number skills can be tested by the familiar arithmetic problem, by checking paired lists of numbers to see which are alike and which are different, or by interpreting charts and graphs. In the latter test, a graph may be printed in the test booklet which you are asked to use as the basis for answering questions.

4) Observation

A popular test for law-enforcement positions is the observation test. A picture is shown to you for several minutes, then taken away. Questions about the picture test your ability to observe both details and larger elements.

5) Following directions

In many positions in the public service, the employee must be able to carry out written instructions dependably and accurately. You may be given a chart with several columns, each column listing a variety of information. The questions require you to carry out directions involving the information given in the chart.

6) Skills and aptitudes

Performance tests effectively measure some manual skills and aptitudes. When the skill is one in which you are trained, such as typing or shorthand, you can practice. These tests are often very much like those given in business school or high school courses. For many of the other skills and aptitudes, however, no short-time preparation can be made. Skills and abilities natural to you or that you have developed throughout your lifetime are being tested.

Many of the general questions just described provide all the data needed to answer the questions and ask you to use your reasoning ability to find the answers. Your best preparation for these tests, as well as for tests of facts and ideas, is to be at your physical and mental best. You, no doubt, have your own methods of getting into an exam-taking mood and keeping "in shape." The next section lists some ideas on this subject.

IV. KINDS OF QUESTIONS

Only rarely is the "essay" question, which you answer in narrative form, used in civil service tests. Civil service tests are usually of the short-answer type. Full instructions for answering these questions will be given to you at the examination. But in case this is your first experience with short-answer questions and separate answer sheets, here is what you need to know:

1) Multiple-choice Questions

Most popular of the short-answer questions is the "multiple choice" or "best answer" question. It can be used, for example, to test for factual knowledge, ability to solve problems or judgment in meeting situations found at work.

A multiple-choice question is normally one of three types—
- It can begin with an incomplete statement followed by several possible endings. You are to find the one ending which *best* completes the statement, although some of the others may not be entirely wrong.
- It can also be a complete statement in the form of a question which is answered by choosing one of the statements listed.

- It can be in the form of a problem – again you select the best answer.

Here is an example of a multiple-choice question with a discussion which should give you some clues as to the method for choosing the right answer:

When an employee has a complaint about his assignment, the action which will *best* help him overcome his difficulty is to
  A. discuss his difficulty with his coworkers
  B. take the problem to the head of the organization
  C. take the problem to the person who gave him the assignment
  D. say nothing to anyone about his complaint

In answering this question, you should study each of the choices to find which is best. Consider choice "A" – Certainly an employee may discuss his complaint with fellow employees, but no change or improvement can result, and the complaint remains unresolved. Choice "B" is a poor choice since the head of the organization probably does not know what assignment you have been given, and taking your problem to him is known as "going over the head" of the supervisor. The supervisor, or person who made the assignment, is the person who can clarify it or correct any injustice. Choice "C" is, therefore, correct. To say nothing, as in choice "D," is unwise. Supervisors have and interest in knowing the problems employees are facing, and the employee is seeking a solution to his problem.

2) True/False Questions

The "true/false" or "right/wrong" form of question is sometimes used. Here a complete statement is given. Your job is to decide whether the statement is right or wrong.

SAMPLE: A roaming cell-phone call to a nearby city costs less than a non-roaming call to a distant city.

This statement is wrong, or false, since roaming calls are more expensive.

This is not a complete list of all possible question forms, although most of the others are variations of these common types. You will always get complete directions for answering questions. Be sure you understand *how* to mark your answers – ask questions until you do.

V. RECORDING YOUR ANSWERS

Computer terminals are used more and more today for many different kinds of exams.

For an examination with very few applicants, you may be told to record your answers in the test booklet itself. Separate answer sheets are much more common. If this separate answer sheet is to be scored by machine – and this is often the case – it is highly important that you mark your answers correctly in order to get credit.

An electronic scoring machine is often used in civil service offices because of the speed with which papers can be scored. Machine-scored answer sheets must be marked with a pencil, which will be given to you. This pencil has a high graphite content which responds to the electronic scoring machine. As a matter of fact, stray dots may register as answers, so do not let your pencil rest on the answer sheet while you are pondering the correct answer. Also, if your pencil lead breaks or is otherwise defective, ask for another.

Since the answer sheet will be dropped in a slot in the scoring machine, be careful not to bend the corners or get the paper crumpled.

The answer sheet normally has five vertical columns of numbers, with 30 numbers to a column. These numbers correspond to the question numbers in your test booklet. After each number, going across the page are four or five pairs of dotted lines. These short dotted lines have small letters or numbers above them. The first two pairs may also have a "T" or "F" above the letters. This indicates that the first two pairs only are to be used if the questions are of the true-false type. If the questions are multiple choice, disregard the "T" and "F" and pay attention only to the small letters or numbers.

Answer your questions in the manner of the sample that follows:

32. The largest city in the United States is
    A. Washington, D.C.
    B. New York City
    C. Chicago
    D. Detroit
    E. San Francisco

1) Choose the answer you think is best. (New York City is the largest, so "B" is correct.)
2) Find the row of dotted lines numbered the same as the question you are answering. (Find row number 32)
3) Find the pair of dotted lines corresponding to the answer. (Find the pair of lines under the mark "B.")
4) Make a solid black mark between the dotted lines.

VI. BEFORE THE TEST

Common sense will help you find procedures to follow to get ready for an examination. Too many of us, however, overlook these sensible measures. Indeed, nervousness and fatigue have been found to be the most serious reasons why applicants fail to do their best on civil service tests. Here is a list of reminders:

- Begin your preparation early – Don't wait until the last minute to go scurrying around for books and materials or to find out what the position is all about.
- Prepare continuously – An hour a night for a week is better than an all-night cram session. This has been definitely established. What is more, a night a week for a month will return better dividends than crowding your study into a shorter period of time.
- Locate the place of the exam – You have been sent a notice telling you when and where to report for the examination. If the location is in a different town or otherwise unfamiliar to you, it would be well to inquire the best route and learn something about the building.
- Relax the night before the test – Allow your mind to rest. Do not study at all that night. Plan some mild recreation or diversion; then go to bed early and get a good night's sleep.
- Get up early enough to make a leisurely trip to the place for the test – This way unforeseen events, traffic snarls, unfamiliar buildings, etc. will not upset you.
- Dress comfortably – A written test is not a fashion show. You will be known by number and not by name, so wear something comfortable.

- Leave excess paraphernalia at home – Shopping bags and odd bundles will get in your way. You need bring only the items mentioned in the official notice you received; usually everything you need is provided. Do not bring reference books to the exam. They will only confuse those last minutes and be taken away from you when in the test room.
- Arrive somewhat ahead of time – If because of transportation schedules you must get there very early, bring a newspaper or magazine to take your mind off yourself while waiting.
- Locate the examination room – When you have found the proper room, you will be directed to the seat or part of the room where you will sit. Sometimes you are given a sheet of instructions to read while you are waiting. Do not fill out any forms until you are told to do so; just read them and be prepared.
- Relax and prepare to listen to the instructions
- If you have any physical problem that may keep you from doing your best, be sure to tell the test administrator. If you are sick or in poor health, you really cannot do your best on the exam. You can come back and take the test some other time.

VII. AT THE TEST

The day of the test is here and you have the test booklet in your hand. The temptation to get going is very strong. Caution! There is more to success than knowing the right answers. You must know how to identify your papers and understand variations in the type of short-answer question used in this particular examination. Follow these suggestions for maximum results from your efforts:

1) Cooperate with the monitor

The test administrator has a duty to create a situation in which you can be as much at ease as possible. He will give instructions, tell you when to begin, check to see that you are marking your answer sheet correctly, and so on. He is not there to guard you, although he will see that your competitors do not take unfair advantage. He wants to help you do your best.

2) Listen to all instructions

Don't jump the gun! Wait until you understand all directions. In most civil service tests you get more time than you need to answer the questions. So don't be in a hurry. Read each word of instructions until you clearly understand the meaning. Study the examples, listen to all announcements and follow directions. Ask questions if you do not understand what to do.

3) Identify your papers

Civil service exams are usually identified by number only. You will be assigned a number; you must not put your name on your test papers. Be sure to copy your number correctly. Since more than one exam may be given, copy your exact examination title.

4) Plan your time

Unless you are told that a test is a "speed" or "rate of work" test, speed itself is usually not important. Time enough to answer all the questions will be provided, but this does not mean that you have all day. An overall time limit has been set. Divide the total time (in minutes) by the number of questions to determine the approximate time you have for each question.

5) Do not linger over difficult questions

If you come across a difficult question, mark it with a paper clip (useful to have along) and come back to it when you have been through the booklet. One caution if you do this – be sure to skip a number on your answer sheet as well. Check often to be sure that you have not lost your place and that you are marking in the row numbered the same as the question you are answering.

6) Read the questions

Be sure you know what the question asks! Many capable people are unsuccessful because they failed to *read* the questions correctly.

7) Answer all questions

Unless you have been instructed that a penalty will be deducted for incorrect answers, it is better to guess than to omit a question.

8) Speed tests

It is often better NOT to guess on speed tests. It has been found that on timed tests people are tempted to spend the last few seconds before time is called in marking answers at random – without even reading them – in the hope of picking up a few extra points. To discourage this practice, the instructions may warn you that your score will be "corrected" for guessing. That is, a penalty will be applied. The incorrect answers will be deducted from the correct ones, or some other penalty formula will be used.

9) Review your answers

If you finish before time is called, go back to the questions you guessed or omitted to give them further thought. Review other answers if you have time.

10) Return your test materials

If you are ready to leave before others have finished or time is called, take ALL your materials to the monitor and leave quietly. Never take any test material with you. The monitor can discover whose papers are not complete, and taking a test booklet may be grounds for disqualification.

VIII. EXAMINATION TECHNIQUES

1) Read the general instructions carefully. These are usually printed on the first page of the exam booklet. As a rule, these instructions refer to the timing of the examination; the fact that you should not start work until the signal and must stop work at a signal, etc. If there are any *special* instructions, such as a choice of questions to be answered, make sure that you note this instruction carefully.

2) When you are ready to start work on the examination, that is as soon as the signal has been given, read the instructions to each question booklet, underline any key words or phrases, such as *least, best, outline, describe* and the like. In this way you will tend to answer as requested rather than discover on reviewing your paper that you *listed without describing*, that you selected the *worst* choice rather than the *best* choice, etc.

3) If the examination is of the objective or multiple-choice type – that is, each question will also give a series of possible answers: A, B, C or D, and you are called upon to select the best answer and write the letter next to that answer on your answer paper – it is advisable to start answering each question in turn. There may be anywhere from 50 to 100 such questions in the three or four hours allotted and you can see how much time would be taken if you read through all the questions before beginning to answer any. Furthermore, if you come across a question or group of questions which you know would be difficult to answer, it would undoubtedly affect your handling of all the other questions.

4) If the examination is of the essay type and contains but a few questions, it is a moot point as to whether you should read all the questions before starting to answer any one. Of course, if you are given a choice – say five out of seven and the like – then it is essential to read all the questions so you can eliminate the two that are most difficult. If, however, you are asked to answer all the questions, there may be danger in trying to answer the easiest one first because you may find that you will spend too much time on it. The best technique is to answer the first question, then proceed to the second, etc.

5) Time your answers. Before the exam begins, write down the time it started, then add the time allowed for the examination and write down the time it must be completed, then divide the time available somewhat as follows:
    - If 3-1/2 hours are allowed, that would be 210 minutes. If you have 80 objective-type questions, that would be an average of 2-1/2 minutes per question. Allow yourself no more than 2 minutes per question, or a total of 160 minutes, which will permit about 50 minutes to review.
    - If for the time allotment of 210 minutes there are 7 essay questions to answer, that would average about 30 minutes a question. Give yourself only 25 minutes per question so that you have about 35 minutes to review.

6) The most important instruction is to *read each question* and make sure you know what is wanted. The second most important instruction is to *time yourself properly* so that you answer every question. The third most important instruction is to *answer every question*. Guess if you have to but include something for each question. Remember that you will receive no credit for a blank and will probably receive some credit if you write something in answer to an essay question. If you guess a letter – say "B" for a multiple-choice question – you may have guessed right. If you leave a blank as an answer to a multiple-choice question, the examiners may respect your feelings but it will not add a point to your score. Some exams may penalize you for wrong answers, so in such cases *only*, you may not want to guess unless you have some basis for your answer.

7) Suggestions
    a. Objective-type questions
        1. Examine the question booklet for proper sequence of pages and questions
        2. Read all instructions carefully
        3. Skip any question which seems too difficult; return to it after all other questions have been answered
        4. Apportion your time properly; do not spend too much time on any single question or group of questions

5. Note and underline key words – *all, most, fewest, least, best, worst, same, opposite,* etc.
6. Pay particular attention to negatives
7. Note unusual option, e.g., unduly long, short, complex, different or similar in content to the body of the question
8. Observe the use of "hedging" words – *probably, may, most likely,* etc.
9. Make sure that your answer is put next to the same number as the question
10. Do not second-guess unless you have good reason to believe the second answer is definitely more correct
11. Cross out original answer if you decide another answer is more accurate; do not erase until you are ready to hand your paper in
12. Answer all questions; guess unless instructed otherwise
13. Leave time for review

b. Essay questions
   1. Read each question carefully
   2. Determine exactly what is wanted. Underline key words or phrases.
   3. Decide on outline or paragraph answer
   4. Include many different points and elements unless asked to develop any one or two points or elements
   5. Show impartiality by giving pros and cons unless directed to select one side only
   6. Make and write down any assumptions you find necessary to answer the questions
   7. Watch your English, grammar, punctuation and choice of words
   8. Time your answers; don't crowd material

8) Answering the essay question

Most essay questions can be answered by framing the specific response around several key words or ideas. Here are a few such key words or ideas:

M's: manpower, materials, methods, money, management
P's: purpose, program, policy, plan, procedure, practice, problems, pitfalls, personnel, public relations

   a. Six basic steps in handling problems:
      1. Preliminary plan and background development
      2. Collect information, data and facts
      3. Analyze and interpret information, data and facts
      4. Analyze and develop solutions as well as make recommendations
      5. Prepare report and sell recommendations
      6. Install recommendations and follow up effectiveness

   b. Pitfalls to avoid
      1. *Taking things for granted* – A statement of the situation does not necessarily imply that each of the elements is necessarily true; for example, a complaint may be invalid and biased so that all that can be taken for granted is that a complaint has been registered

2. *Considering only one side of a situation* – Wherever possible, indicate several alternatives and then point out the reasons you selected the best one
3. *Failing to indicate follow up* – Whenever your answer indicates action on your part, make certain that you will take proper follow-up action to see how successful your recommendations, procedures or actions turn out to be
4. *Taking too long in answering any single question* – Remember to time your answers properly

IX. AFTER THE TEST

Scoring procedures differ in detail among civil service jurisdictions although the general principles are the same. Whether the papers are hand-scored or graded by machine we have described, they are nearly always graded by number. That is, the person who marks the paper knows only the number – never the name – of the applicant. Not until all the papers have been graded will they be matched with names. If other tests, such as training and experience or oral interview ratings have been given, scores will be combined. Different parts of the examination usually have different weights. For example, the written test might count 60 percent of the final grade, and a rating of training and experience 40 percent. In many jurisdictions, veterans will have a certain number of points added to their grades.

After the final grade has been determined, the names are placed in grade order and an eligible list is established. There are various methods for resolving ties between those who get the same final grade – probably the most common is to place first the name of the person whose application was received first. Job offers are made from the eligible list in the order the names appear on it. You will be notified of your grade and your rank as soon as all these computations have been made. This will be done as rapidly as possible.

People who are found to meet the requirements in the announcement are called "eligibles." Their names are put on a list of eligible candidates. An eligible's chances of getting a job depend on how high he stands on this list and how fast agencies are filling jobs from the list.

When a job is to be filled from a list of eligibles, the agency asks for the names of people on the list of eligibles for that job. When the civil service commission receives this request, it sends to the agency the names of the three people highest on this list. Or, if the job to be filled has specialized requirements, the office sends the agency the names of the top three persons who meet these requirements from the general list.

The appointing officer makes a choice from among the three people whose names were sent to him. If the selected person accepts the appointment, the names of the others are put back on the list to be considered for future openings.

That is the rule in hiring from all kinds of eligible lists, whether they are for typist, carpenter, chemist, or something else. For every vacancy, the appointing officer has his choice of any one of the top three eligibles on the list. This explains why the person whose name is on top of the list sometimes does not get an appointment when some of the persons lower on the list do. If the appointing officer chooses the second or third eligible, the No. 1 eligible does not get a job at once, but stays on the list until he is appointed or the list is terminated.

X. HOW TO PASS THE INTERVIEW TEST

The examination for which you applied requires an oral interview test. You have already taken the written test and you are now being called for the interview test – the final part of the formal examination.

You may think that it is not possible to prepare for an interview test and that there are no procedures to follow during an interview. Our purpose is to point out some things you can do in advance that will help you and some good rules to follow and pitfalls to avoid while you are being interviewed.

What is an interview supposed to test?

The written examination is designed to test the technical knowledge and competence of the candidate; the oral is designed to evaluate intangible qualities, not readily measured otherwise, and to establish a list showing the relative fitness of each candidate – as measured against his competitors – for the position sought. Scoring is not on the basis of "right" and "wrong," but on a sliding scale of values ranging from "not passable" to "outstanding." As a matter of fact, it is possible to achieve a relatively low score without a single "incorrect" answer because of evident weakness in the qualities being measured.

Occasionally, an examination may consist entirely of an oral test – either an individual or a group oral. In such cases, information is sought concerning the technical knowledges and abilities of the candidate, since there has been no written examination for this purpose. More commonly, however, an oral test is used to supplement a written examination.

Who conducts interviews?

The composition of oral boards varies among different jurisdictions. In nearly all, a representative of the personnel department serves as chairman. One of the members of the board may be a representative of the department in which the candidate would work. In some cases, "outside experts" are used, and, frequently, a businessman or some other representative of the general public is asked to serve. Labor and management or other special groups may be represented. The aim is to secure the services of experts in the appropriate field.

However the board is composed, it is a good idea (and not at all improper or unethical) to ascertain in advance of the interview who the members are and what groups they represent. When you are introduced to them, you will have some idea of their backgrounds and interests, and at least you will not stutter and stammer over their names.

What should be done before the interview?

While knowledge about the board members is useful and takes some of the surprise element out of the interview, there is other preparation which is more substantive. It *is* possible to prepare for an oral interview – in several ways:

1) Keep a copy of your application and review it carefully before the interview

This may be the only document before the oral board, and the starting point of the interview. Know what education and experience you have listed there, and the sequence and dates of all of it. Sometimes the board will ask you to review the highlights of your experience for them; you should not have to hem and haw doing it.

2) Study the class specification and the examination announcement

Usually, the oral board has one or both of these to guide them. The qualities, characteristics or knowledges required by the position sought are stated in these documents. They offer valuable clues as to the nature of the oral interview. For example, if the job involves supervisory responsibilities, the announcement will usually indicate that knowledge of modern supervisory methods and the qualifications of the candidate as a supervisor will be tested. If so, you can expect such questions, frequently in the form of a hypothetical situation which you are expected to solve. NEVER go into an oral without knowledge of the duties and responsibilities of the job you seek.

3) Think through each qualification required

Try to visualize the kind of questions you would ask if you were a board member. How well could you answer them? Try especially to appraise your own knowledge and background in each area, *measured against the job sought*, and identify any areas in which you are weak. Be critical and realistic – do not flatter yourself.

4) Do some general reading in areas in which you feel you may be weak

For example, if the job involves supervision and your past experience has NOT, some general reading in supervisory methods and practices, particularly in the field of human relations, might be useful. Do NOT study agency procedures or detailed manuals. The oral board will be testing your understanding and capacity, not your memory.

5) Get a good night's sleep and watch your general health and mental attitude

You will want a clear head at the interview. Take care of a cold or any other minor ailment, and of course, no hangovers.

What should be done on the day of the interview?

Now comes the day of the interview itself. Give yourself plenty of time to get there. Plan to arrive somewhat ahead of the scheduled time, particularly if your appointment is in the fore part of the day. If a previous candidate fails to appear, the board might be ready for you a bit early. By early afternoon an oral board is almost invariably behind schedule if there are many candidates, and you may have to wait. Take along a book or magazine to read, or your application to review, but leave any extraneous material in the waiting room when you go in for your interview. In any event, relax and compose yourself.

The matter of dress is important. The board is forming impressions about you – from your experience, your manners, your attitude, and your appearance. Give your personal appearance careful attention. Dress your best, but not your flashiest. Choose conservative, appropriate clothing, and be sure it is immaculate. This is a business interview, and your appearance should indicate that you regard it as such. Besides, being well groomed and properly dressed will help boost your confidence.

Sooner or later, someone will call your name and escort you into the interview room. *This is it.* From here on you are on your own. It is too late for any more preparation. But remember, you asked for this opportunity to prove your fitness, and you are here because your request was granted.

What happens when you go in?

The usual sequence of events will be as follows: The clerk (who is often the board stenographer) will introduce you to the chairman of the oral board, who will introduce you to the other members of the board. Acknowledge the introductions before you sit down. Do not be surprised if you find a microphone facing you or a stenotypist sitting by. Oral interviews are usually recorded in the event of an appeal or other review.

Usually the chairman of the board will open the interview by reviewing the highlights of your education and work experience from your application – primarily for the benefit of the other members of the board, as well as to get the material into the record. Do not interrupt or comment unless there is an error or significant misinterpretation; if that is the case, do not hesitate. But do not quibble about insignificant matters. Also, he will usually ask you some question about your education, experience or your present job – partly to get you to start talking and to establish the interviewing "rapport." He may start the actual questioning, or turn it over to one of the other members. Frequently, each member undertakes the questioning on a particular area, one in which he is perhaps most competent, so you can expect each member to participate in the examination. Because time is limited, you may also expect some rather abrupt switches in the direction the questioning takes, so do not be upset by it. Normally, a board member will not pursue a single line of questioning unless he discovers a particular strength or weakness.

After each member has participated, the chairman will usually ask whether any member has any further questions, then will ask you if you have anything you wish to add. Unless you are expecting this question, it may floor you. Worse, it may start you off on an extended, extemporaneous speech. The board is not usually seeking more information. The question is principally to offer you a last opportunity to present further qualifications or to indicate that you have nothing to add. So, if you feel that a significant qualification or characteristic has been overlooked, it is proper to point it out in a sentence or so. Do not compliment the board on the thoroughness of their examination – they have been sketchy, and you know it. If you wish, merely say, "No thank you, I have nothing further to add." This is a point where you can "talk yourself out" of a good impression or fail to present an important bit of information. Remember, *you close the interview yourself*.

The chairman will then say, "That is all, Mr. _____, thank you." Do not be startled; the interview is over, and quicker than you think. Thank him, gather your belongings and take your leave. Save your sigh of relief for the other side of the door.

How to put your best foot forward

Throughout this entire process, you may feel that the board individually and collectively is trying to pierce your defenses, seek out your hidden weaknesses and embarrass and confuse you. Actually, this is not true. They are obliged to make an appraisal of your qualifications for the job you are seeking, and they want to see you in your best light. Remember, they must interview all candidates and a non-cooperative candidate may become a failure in spite of their best efforts to bring out his qualifications. Here are 15 suggestions that will help you:

1) Be natural – Keep your attitude confident, not cocky

If you are not confident that you can do the job, do not expect the board to be. Do not apologize for your weaknesses, try to bring out your strong points. The board is interested in a positive, not negative, presentation. Cockiness will antagonize any board member and make him wonder if you are covering up a weakness by a false show of strength.

2) Get comfortable, but don't lounge or sprawl

Sit erectly but not stiffly. A careless posture may lead the board to conclude that you are careless in other things, or at least that you are not impressed by the importance of the occasion. Either conclusion is natural, even if incorrect. Do not fuss with your clothing, a pencil or an ashtray. Your hands may occasionally be useful to emphasize a point; do not let them become a point of distraction.

3) Do not wisecrack or make small talk

This is a serious situation, and your attitude should show that you consider it as such. Further, the time of the board is limited – they do not want to waste it, and neither should you.

4) Do not exaggerate your experience or abilities

In the first place, from information in the application or other interviews and sources, the board may know more about you than you think. Secondly, you probably will not get away with it. An experienced board is rather adept at spotting such a situation, so do not take the chance.

5) If you know a board member, do not make a point of it, yet do not hide it

Certainly you are not fooling him, and probably not the other members of the board. Do not try to take advantage of your acquaintanceship – it will probably do you little good.

6) Do not dominate the interview

Let the board do that. They will give you the clues – do not assume that you have to do all the talking. Realize that the board has a number of questions to ask you, and do not try to take up all the interview time by showing off your extensive knowledge of the answer to the first one.

7) Be attentive

You only have 20 minutes or so, and you should keep your attention at its sharpest throughout. When a member is addressing a problem or question to you, give him your undivided attention. Address your reply principally to him, but do not exclude the other board members.

8) Do not interrupt

A board member may be stating a problem for you to analyze. He will ask you a question when the time comes. Let him state the problem, and wait for the question.

9) Make sure you understand the question

Do not try to answer until you are sure what the question is. If it is not clear, restate it in your own words or ask the board member to clarify it for you. However, do not haggle about minor elements.

10) Reply promptly but not hastily

A common entry on oral board rating sheets is "candidate responded readily," or "candidate hesitated in replies." Respond as promptly and quickly as you can, but do not jump to a hasty, ill-considered answer.

11) Do not be peremptory in your answers

A brief answer is proper – but do not fire your answer back. That is a losing game from your point of view. The board member can probably ask questions much faster than you can answer them.

12) Do not try to create the answer you think the board member wants

He is interested in what kind of mind you have and how it works – not in playing games. Furthermore, he can usually spot this practice and will actually grade you down on it.

13) Do not switch sides in your reply merely to agree with a board member

Frequently, a member will take a contrary position merely to draw you out and to see if you are willing and able to defend your point of view. Do not start a debate, yet do not surrender a good position. If a position is worth taking, it is worth defending.

14) Do not be afraid to admit an error in judgment if you are shown to be wrong

The board knows that you are forced to reply without any opportunity for careful consideration. Your answer may be demonstrably wrong. If so, admit it and get on with the interview.

15) Do not dwell at length on your present job

The opening question may relate to your present assignment. Answer the question but do not go into an extended discussion. You are being examined for a *new* job, not your present one. As a matter of fact, try to phrase ALL your answers in terms of the job for which you are being examined.

Basis of Rating

Probably you will forget most of these "do's" and "don'ts" when you walk into the oral interview room. Even remembering them all will not ensure you a passing grade. Perhaps you did not have the qualifications in the first place. But remembering them will help you to put your best foot forward, without treading on the toes of the board members.

Rumor and popular opinion to the contrary notwithstanding, an oral board wants you to make the best appearance possible. They know you are under pressure – but they also want to see how you respond to it as a guide to what your reaction would be under the pressures of the job you seek. They will be influenced by the degree of poise you display, the personal traits you show and the manner in which you respond.

ABOUT THIS BOOK

This book contains tests divided into Examination Sections. Go through each test, answering every question in the margin. We have also attached a sample answer sheet at the back of the book that can be removed and used. At the end of each test look at the answer key and check your answers. On the ones you got wrong, look at the right answer choice and learn. Do not fill in the answers first. Do not memorize the questions and answers, but understand the answer and principles involved. On your test, the questions will likely be different from the samples. Questions are changed and new ones added. If you understand these past questions you should have success with any changes that arise. Tests may consist of several types of questions. We have additional books on each subject should more study be advisable or necessary for you. Finally, the more you study, the better prepared you will be. This book is intended to be the last thing you study before you walk into the examination room. Prior study of relevant texts is also recommended. NLC publishes some of these in our Fundamental Series. Knowledge and good sense are important factors in passing your exam. Good luck also helps. So now study this Passbook, absorb the material contained within and take that knowledge into the examination. Then do your best to pass that exam.

EXAMINATION SECTION

EXAMINATION SECTION
TEST 1

DIRECTIONS: Each question or incomplete statement is followed by several suggested answers or completions. Select the one that BEST answers the question or completes the statement. *PRINT THE LETTER OF THE CORRECT ANSWER IN THE SPACE AT THE RIGHT.*

Questions 1-5.

DIRECTIONS: Questions 1 through 5 consist of a sentence with an underlined word. For each question, select the choice that is CLOSEST in meaning to the underlined word.

EXAMPLE
This division reviews the fiscal reports of the agency.
In this sentence, the word *fiscal* means MOST NEARLY
    A. financial   B. critical   C. basic   D. personnel
The correct answer is A. "financial" because "financial" is closest to *fiscal*. Therefore, the answer is A.

1. Every good office worker needs basic skills.
   The word *basic* in this sentence means
     A. fundamental B. advanced C. unusual D. outstanding

2. He turned out to be a good instructor.
   The word *instructor* in this sentence means
     A. student B. worker C. typist D. teacher

3. The quantity of work in the office was under study.
   In this sentence, the word *quantity* means
     A. amount B. flow C. supervision D. type

4. The morning was spent examining the time records.
   In this sentence, the word *examining* means
     A. distributing B. collecting C. checking D. filing

5. The candidate filled in the proper spaces on the form.
   In this sentence, the word *proper* means
     A. blank B. appropriate C. many D. remaining

Questions 6-8.

DIRECTIONS: Questions 6 through 8 are to be answered SOLELY on the basis of the information contained in the following paragraph.

The increase in the number of public documents in the last two centuries closely matches the increase in population in the United States. The great number of public documents has become a serious threat to their usefulness. It is necessary to have programs which will reduce the number of public documents that are kept and which will, at the same time, assure keeping those that have value. Such programs need a great deal of thought to have any success.

6. According to the above paragraph, public documents may be less useful if 6.____
   A. the files are open to the public
   B. the record room is too small
   C. the copying machine is operated only during normal working hours
   D. too many records are being kept

7. According to the above paragraph, the growth of the population in the United 7.____
   States has matched the growth in the quantity of public documents for a period of MOST NEARLY _____ years.
   A. 50   B. 100   C. 200   D. 300

8. According to the above paragraph, the increased number of public documents 8.____
   has made it necessary to
   A. find out which public documents are worth keeping
   B. reduce the great number of public documents by decreasing government services
   C. eliminate the copying of all original public documents
   D. avoid all new copying devices

Questions 9-10.

DIRECTIONS: Questions 9 and 10 are to be answered SOLELY on the basis of the information contained in the following paragraph.

The work goals of an agency can best be reached if the employees understand and agree with these goals. One way to gain such understanding and agreement is for management to encourage and seriously consider suggestions from employees in the setting of agency goals.

9. On the basis of the above paragraph, the BEST way to achieve the work goals 9.____
   of an agency is to
   A. make certain that employees work as hard as possible
   B. study the organizational structure of the agency
   C. encourage employees to think seriously about the agency's problems
   D. stimulate employee understanding of the work goals

10. On the basis of the above paragraph, understanding and agreement with agency   10.____
    goals can be gained by
    A. allowing the employees to set agency goals
    B. reaching agency goals quickly
    C. legislative review of agency operations
    D. employee participation in setting agency goals

Questions 11-15.

DIRECTIONS: Each of Questions 11 through 15 consists of a group of four words. One word in each group is incorrectly spelled. For each question, print the letter of the correct answer in the space at the right that is the same as the letter next to the word which is INCORRECTLY spelled.

EXAMPLE

A. housing   B. certain   C. budgit   D. money

The word "budgit" is incorrectly spelled, because the correct spelling should be "budget." Therefore, the correct answer is C.

11.	A. sentince	B. bulletin	C. notice	D. definition	11.____
12.	A. appointment	B. exactly	C. typest	D. light	12.____
13.	A. penalty	B. suparvise	C. consider	D. division	13.____
14.	A. schedule	B. accurate	C. corect	D. simple	14.____
15.	A. suggestion	B. installed	C. proper	D. agincy	15.____

Questions 16-20.

DIRECTIONS: Each Question 16 through 20 consists of a sentence which may be
A. incorrect because of bad word usage, or
B. incorrect because of bad punctuation, or
C. incorrect because of bad spelling, or
D. correct
Read each sentence carefully. Then print in the space at the right A, B, C, or D, according to the answer you choose from the four choices listed above. There is only one type of error in each incorrect sentence. If there is no error, the sentence is correct.

EXAMPLE

George Washington was the father of his contry.
This sentence is incorrect because of bad spelling ("contry" instead of "country").
Therefore, the answer is C.

16. The assignment was completed in record time but the payroll for it has not yet been preparid. 16.____

17. The operator, on the other hand, is willing to learn me how to use the mimeograph. 17.____

18. She is the prettiest of the three sisters. 18.____

19. She doesn't know; if the mail has arrived. 19.____

20. The doorknob of the office door is broke. 20.____

21. A clerk can process a form in 15 minutes.
    How many forms can that clerk process in six hours?
    A. 10   B. 21   C. 24   D. 90   21.____

22. An office staff consists of 120 people. Sixty of them have been assigned to a special project. Of the remaining staff, 20 answer the mail, 10 handle phone calls, and the rest operate the office machines.
    The number of people operating the office machines is
    A. 20   B. 30   C. 40   D. 45   22.____

23. An office worker received 65 applications but on the first day had to return 26 of them for being incomplete and on the second day 25 had to be returned for being incomplete.
    How many applications did NOT have to be returned?
    A. 10   B. 12   C. 14   D. 16   23.____

24. An office worker answered 63 phone calls in one day and 91 phone calls the next day.
    For these 2 days, what was the average number of phone calls he answered per day?
    A. 77   B. 28   C. 82   D. 93   24.____

25. An office worker processed 12 vouchers of $8.50 each, 3 vouchers of $3.68 each, and 2 vouchers of $1.29 each.
    The TOTAL dollar amount of these vouchers is
    A. $116.04   B. $117.52   C. $118.62   D. $119.04   25.____

KEY (CORRECT ANSWERS)

1.	A		11.	A
2.	D		12.	C
3.	A		13.	B
4.	C		14.	C
5.	B		15.	D
6.	D		16.	C
7.	C		17.	A
8.	A		18.	D
9.	D		19.	B
10.	D		20.	A

21. C
22. B
23. C
24. A
25. C

TEST 2

DIRECTIONS: Each question or incomplete statement is followed by several suggested answers or completions. Select the one that BEST answers the question or completes the statement. *PRINT THE LETTER OF THE CORRECT ANSWER IN THE SPACE AT THE RIGHT.*

Questions 1-5.

DIRECTIONS: Each Question from 1 through 5 lists four names. The names may not be exactly the same. Compare the names in each question and mark your answer
- A if all the names are different
- B if only two names are exactly the same
- C if only three names are exactly the same
- D if all four names are exactly the same

EXAMPLE
Jensen, Alfred E.
Jensen, Alfred E.
Jensan, Alfred E.
Jensen, Fred E.

Since the name Jensen, Alfred E. appears twice and is exactly the same in both places, the correct answer is B.

1. A. Riviera, Pedro S.   B. Rivers, Pedro S.   1.____
   C. Riviera, Pedro N.   D. Riviera, Juan S.

2. A. Guider, Albert   B. Guidar, Albert   2.____
   C. Giuder, Alfred   D. Guider, Albert

3. A. Blum, Rona   B. Blum, Rona   3.____
   C. Blum, Rona   D. Blum, Rona

4. A. Raugh, John   B. Raugh, James   4.____
   C. Raughe, John   D. Raugh, John

5. A. Katz, Stanley   B. Katz, Stanley   5.____
   C. Katze, Stanley   D. Katz, Stanley

Questions 6-10.

DIRECTIONS: Each Question 6 through 10 consists of numbers or letters in Columns I and II. For each question, compare each line of Column I with its corresponding line in Column II and decide how many lines in Column I are EXACTLY the same as their corresponding lines in Column II. In your answer space, mark your answer
- A if only ONE line in Column I is exactly the same as its corresponding line in Column II
- B if only TWO lines in Column I are exactly the same as their corresponding lines in Column II

2 (#2)

C if only THREE lines in Column I are exactly the same as their corresponding lines in Column II
D if all FOUR lines in Column I are exactly the same as their corresponding lines in Column II

EXAMPLE

Column I	Column II
1776	1776
1865	1865
1945	1945
1976	1978

Only three lines in Column I are exactly the same as their corresponding lines in Column II. Therefore, the correct answer is C.

	Column I	Column II	
6.	5653	5653	6.___
	8727	8728	
	ZPSS	ZPSS	
	4952	9453	
7.	PNJP	PNPJ	7.___
	NJPJ	NJPJ	
	JNPN	JNPN	
	PNJP	PNPJ	
8.	effe	eFfe	8.___
	uWvw	uWvw	
	KpGj	KpGg	
	vmnv	vmnv	
9.	5232	5232	9.___
	PfrC	PfrN	
	zssz	zzss	
	rwwr	rwww	
10.	czws	czws	10.___
	cecc	cece	
	thrm	thrm	
	lwtz	lwtz	

Questions 11-15.

DIRECTIONS: Questions 11 through 15 have lines of letters and numbers. Each letter should be matched with its number in accordance with the following table.

Letter	F	R	C	A	W	L	E	N	B	T
Matching Number	0	1	2	3	4	5	6	7	8	9

From the table you can determine that the letter F has the matching number 0 below it, the letter R has the matching number 1 below, etc.

For each question, compare each line of letters and numbers carefully to see if each letter has its correct matching number. If all the letters and numbers are matched correctly in

  none of the lines of the question, mark your answer A
  only *one* of the lines of the question, mark your answer B
  only *two* of the lines of the question, mark your answer C
  all three lines of the question, mark your answer D

EXAMPLE

    WBCR   4826
    TLBF   9580
    ATNE   3986

There is a mistake in the first line because the letter R should have its matching number 1 instead of the number 6.

The second line is correct because each letter shown has the correct matching number.

There is a mistake in the third line because the letter N should have the matching number 7 instead of the number 8.

Since all the letters and numbers are correct matched in only one of the lines in the sample, the correct answer is B.

11. EBCT   6829   11.____
    ATWR   3961
    NLBW   7584

12. RNCT   1729   12.____
    LNCR   5728
    WAEB   5368

13. NTWB   7948   13.____
    RABL   1385
    TAEF   9360

14. LWRB   5417   14.____
    RLWN   1647
    CBWA   2843

15. ABTC   3792   15.____
    WCER   5261
    AWCN   3417

16. Your job often brings you into contact with the public.   16.____
    Of the following, it would be MOST desirable to explain the reasons for official actions to people coming into your office for assistance because such explanations
    A. help build greater understanding between the public and your agency
    B. help build greater self-confidence in city employees
    C. convince the public that nothing they do can upset a city employee
    D. show the public that city employees are intelligent

17. Assume that you strongly dislike one of your co-workers.
    You should FIRST
    A. discuss your feeling with the co-worker
    B. demand a transfer to another office
    C. suggest to your supervisor that the co-worker should be observed carefully
    D. try to figure out the reason for this dislike before you say or do anything

18. An office worker who has problems accepting authority is MOST likely to find it difficult to
    A. obey rules
    B. understand people
    C. assist other employees
    D. follow complex instructions

19. The employees in your office have taken a dislike to one person and frequently annoy her.
    Your supervisor should
    A. transfer this person to another unit at the first opportunity
    B. try to find out the reason for the staff's attitude before doing anything about it
    C. threaten to transfer the first person observed bothering this person
    D. ignore the situation

20. Assume that your supervisor has asked a worker in your office to get a copy of a report out of the files. You notice the worker as accidentally pulled out the wrong report.
    Of the following, the BEST way for you to handle this situation is to tell
    A. the worker about all the difficulties that will result from this error
    B. the worker about her mistake in a nice way
    C. the worker to ignore this error
    D. your supervisor that this worker needs more training in how to use the files

21. Filing systems differ in their efficiency.
    Which of the following is the BEST way to evaluate the efficiency of a filing system? A
    A. number of times used per day
    B. amount of material that is received each day for filing
    C. amount of time it takes to locate material
    D. type of locking system used

22. In planning ahead so that a sufficient amount of general office supplies is always available, it would be LEAST important to find out the
    A. current office supply needs of the staff
    B. amount of office supplies used last year
    C. days and times that office supplies can be ordered
    D. agency goals and objectives

23. The MAIN reason for establishing routine office work procedures is that once a routine is established
    A. work need not be checked for accuracy
    B. all steps in the routine will take an equal amount of time to perform
    C. each time the job is repeated, it will take less time to perform
    D. each step in the routine will not have to be planned all over again each time

24. When an office machine centrally located in an agency must be shut down for repairs, the bureaus and divisions using this machine should be informed of the
    A. expected length of time before the machine will be in operation again
    B. estimated cost of repairs
    C. efforts being made to avoid future repairs
    D. type of new equipment which the agency may buy in the future to replace the machine being repaired

25. If the day's work is properly scheduled, the MOST important result would be that the
    A. supervisor will not have to do much supervision
    B. employee will know what to do next
    C. employee will show greater initiative
    D. job will become routine

KEY (CORRECT ANSWERS)

1.	A		11.	C
2.	B		12.	B
3.	D		13.	D
4.	B		14.	B
5.	C		15.	A
6.	B		16.	A
7.	B		17.	D
8.	B		18.	A
9.	A		19.	B
10.	C		20.	B

21. C
22. D
23. D
24. A
25. B

EXAMINATION SECTION
TEST 1

DIRECTIONS: Each question or incomplete statement is followed by several suggested answers or completions. Select the one that BEST answers the question or completes the statement. *PRINT THE LETTER OF THE CORRECT ANSWER IN THE SPACE AT THE RIGHT.*

Questions 1-10.

WORD MEANING

DIRECTIONS: Each question from 1 to 10 contains a word in capitals followed by four suggested meanings of the word. For each question, choose the best meaning. *PRINT THE LETTER OF THE CORRECT ANSWER IN THE SPACE AT THE RIGHT.*

1. ACCURATE
   A. correct   B. useful   C. afraid   D. careless

2. ALTER
   A. copy   B. change   C. report   D. agree

3. DOCUMENT
   A. outline   B. agreement   C. blueprint   D. record

4. INDICATE
   A. listen   B. show   C. guess   D. try

5. INVENTORY
   A. custom   B. discovery   C. warning   D. list

6. ISSUE
   A. annoy   B. use up   C. give out   D. gain

7. NOTIFY
   A. inform   B. promise   C. approve   D. strengthen

8. ROUTINE
   A. path   B. mistake   C. habit   D. journey

9. TERMINATE
   A. rest   B. start   C. deny   D. end

10. TRANSMIT
    A. put in   B. send   C. stop   D. go across

Questions 11-15.

READING COMPREHENSION

DIRECTIONS: Questions 11 through 15 test how well you understand what you read. It will be necessary for you to read carefully because your answers to these questions should be based ONLY on the information given in the following paragraphs.

The recipient gains an impression of a typewritten letter before he begins to read the message. Pastors which provide for a good first impression include margins and spacing that are visually pleasing, formal parts of the letter which are correctly placed according to the style of the letter, copy which is free of obvious erasures and over-strikes, and transcript that is even and clear. The problem for the typist is that of how to produce that first, positive impression of her work.

There are several general rules which a typist can follow when she wishes to prepare a properly spaced letter on a sheet of letter-head. Ordinarily, the width of a letter should not be less than four inches nor more than six inches. The side margins should also have a desirable relation to the bottom margin and the space between the letterhead and the body of the letter. Usually the most appealing arrangement is when the side margins are even and the bottom margin is slightly wider than the side margins. In some offices, however, standard line length is used for all business letters, and the secretary then varies the spacing between the date line and the inside address according to the length of the letter.

11. The BEST title for the above paragraphs would be:

    A. Writing Office Letters
    B. Making Good First Impressions
    C. Judging Well-Typed Letters
    D. Good Placing and Spacing for Office Letters

12. According to the above paragraphs, which of the following might be considered the way in which people very quickly judge the quality of work which has been typed? By

    A. measuring the margins to see if they are correct
    B. looking at the spacing and cleanliness of the typescript
    C. scanning the body of the letter for meaning
    D. reading the date line and address for errors

13. What, according to the above paragraphs, would be definitely UNDESIRABLE as the average line length of a typed letter?

    A. 4"   B. 5"   C. 6"   D. 7"

14. According to the above paragraphs, when the line length is kept standard, the secretary

    A. does not have to vary the spacing at all since this also is standard
    B. adjusts the spacing between the date line and inside address for different lengths of letters
    C. uses the longest line as a guideline for spacing between the date line and inside address
    D. varies the number of spaces between the lines

15. According to the above paragraphs, side margins are MOST pleasing when they 15.____
   A. are even and somewhat smaller than the bottom margin
   B. are slightly wider than the bottom margin
   C. vary with the length of the letter
   D. are figured independently from the letterhead and the body of the letter

Questions 16-20.

CODING

DIRECTIONS:

```
Name of Applicant    H A N G S B R U K E
Test Code            c o m p l e x i t y
File Number          0 1 2 3 4 5 6 7 8 9
```

Assume that each of the above capital letters is the first letter of the name of an Applicant, that the small letter directly beneath each capital letter is the test code for the Applicant, and that the number directly beneath each code letter is the file number for the Applicant.

In each of the following Questions 16 through 20, the test code letters and the file numbers in Columns 2 and 3 should correspond to the capital letters in Column 1. For each question, look at each column carefully and mark your answer as follows:

If there is an error only in Column 2, mark your answer A.
If there is an error only in Column 3, mark your answer B.
If there is an error in both Columns 2 and 3, mark your answer C.
If both Columns 2 and 3 are correct, mark your answer D.

The following sample question is given to help you understand the procedure.

SAMPLE QUESTION

Column 1	Column 2	Column 3
AKEHN	otyci	18902

In Column 2, the final test code letter *i.* should be *m*. Column 3 is correctly coded to Column 1. Since there is an error only in Column 2, the answer is A.

	Column 1	Column 2	Column 3	
16.	NEKKU	mytti	29987	16.____
17.	KRAEB	txyle	86095	17.____
18.	ENAUK	ymoit	92178	18.____
19.	REANA	xeomo	69121	19.____
20.	EKHSE	ytcxy	97049	20.____

Questions 21-30.

ARITHMETICAL REASONING

21. If a secretary answered 28 phone calls and typed the addresses for 112 credit statements in one morning, what is the ratio of phone calls answered to credit statements typed for that period of time?

    A. 1:4   B. 1:7   C. 2:3   D. 3:5

22. According to a suggested filing system, no more than 10 folders should be filed behind any one file guide and from 15 to 25 file guides should be used in each file drawer for easy finding and filing.
    The maximum number of folders that a five-drawer file cabinet can hold to allow easy finding and filing is

    A. 550   B. 750   C. 1,100   D. 1,250

23. An employee had a starting salary of $25,804. He received a salary increase at the end of each year, and at the end of the seventh year his salary was $33,476.
    What was his average annual increase in salary over these seven years?

    A. $1,020   B. $1,076   C. $1,096   D. $1,144

24. The 55 typists and 28 senior clerks in a certain city agency were paid a total of $1,943,200 in salaries last year.
    If the average annual salary of a typist was $22,400 the average annual salary of a senior clerk was

    A. $25,400   B. $26,600   C. $26,800   D. $27,000

25. A typist has been given a three page report to type. She has finished typing the first two pages. The first page has 283 words, and the second page has 366 words.
    If the total report consists of 954 words, how many words will she have to type on the third page of the report?

    A. 202   B. 287   C. 305   D. 313

26. In one day, Clerk A processed 30% more forms than Clerk B, and Clerk C processed 1¼ times as many forms as Clerk A. If Clerk B processed 40 forms, how many more forms were processed by Clerk C than Clerk B?

    A. 12   B. 13   C. 21   D. 25

27. A clerk who earns a gross salary of $452 every two weeks has the following deductions taken from her paycheck:
    15% for City, State, Federal taxes; 2 1/2% for Social Security; $1.30 for health insurance; and $6.00 for union dues. The amount of her take-home pay is

    A. $256.20   B. $312.40   C. $331.60   D. $365.60

28. In 2005, a city agency spent $2,000 to buy pencils at a cost of $5.00 a dozen.
    If the agency used 3/4 of these pencils in 2005 and used the same number of pencils in 2006, how many more pencils did it have to buy to have enough pencils for all of 2006?

    A. 1,200   B. 2,400   C. 3,600   D. 4,800

29. A clerk who worked in Agency X earned the following salaries: $20,140 the first year, $21,000 the second year, and $21,920 the third year. Another clerk who worked in Agency Y for three years earned $21,100 a year for two years and $21,448 the third year. The difference between the average salaries received by both clerks over a three-year period is

   A. $196 B. $204 C. $348 D. $564

30. An employee who works over 40 hours in any week receives overtime payment for the extra hours at time and one-half (1 1/2 times) his hourly rate of pay. An employee who earns $13.60 an hour works a total of 45 hours during a certain week.
   His total pay for that week would be

   A. $564.40 B. $612.00 C. $646.00 D. $812.00

Questions 31-35.

RELATED INFORMATION

31. To tell a newly-employed clerk to fill a top drawer of a four-drawer cabinet with heavy folders which will be often used and to keep lower drawers only partly filled is

   A. *good,* because a tall person would have to bend unnecessarily if he had to use a lower drawer
   B. *bad,* because the file cabinet may tip over when the top drawer is opened
   C. *good,* because it is the most easily reachable drawer for the average person
   D. *bad,* because a person bending down at another drawer may accidentally bang his head on the bottom of the drawer when he straightens up

32. If a senior typist or senior clerk has requisitioned a *ream* of paper in order to duplicate a single page office announcement, how many announcements can be printed from the one package of paper?

   A. 200 B. 500 C. 700 D. 1,000

33. Your supervisor has asked you to locate a telephone number for an attorney named Jones, whose office is located at 311 Broadway, and whose name is not already listed in your files.
   The BEST method for finding the number would be for you to

   A. call the information operator and have her get it for you
   B. look in the alphabetical directory (white pages) under the name Jones at 311 Broadway
   C. refer to the heading Attorney in the yellow pages for the name Jones at 311 Broadway
   D. ask your supervisor who referred her to Mr. Jones, then call that person for the number

34. An example of material that should NOT be sent by first class mail is a

   A. email copy of a letter   B. post card
   C. business reply card   D. large catalogue

35. In the operations of a government agency, a voucher is ORDINARILY used to   35.____
    A. refer someone to the agency for a position or assignment
    B. certify that an agency's records of financial trans-actions are accurate
    C. order payment from agency funds of a stated amount to an individual
    D. enter a statement of official opinion in the records of the agency

Questions 36-40.

ENGLISH USAGE

DIRECTIONS: Each question from 36 through 40 contains a sentence. Read each sentence carefully to decide whether it is correct. Then, in the space at the right, mark your answer:

(A) if the sentence is incorrect because of bad grammar or sentence structure

(B) if the sentence is incorrect because of bad punctuation

(C) if the sentence is incorrect because of bad capitalization

(D) if the sentence is correct

Each incorrect sentence has only one type of error. Consider a sentence correct if it has no errors, although there may be other correct ways of saying the same thing.

SAMPLE QUESTION I: One of our clerks were promoted yesterday.

The subject of this sentence is *one,* so the verb should be *was promoted* instead of *were promoted.* Since the sentence is incorrect because of bad grammar, the answer to Sample Question I is (A).

SAMPLE QUESTION II: Between you and me, I would prefer not going there.

Since this sentence is correct, the answer to Sample Question II is (D).

36. The National alliance of Businessmen is trying to persuade private businesses to hire youth in the summertime.   36.____

37. The supervisor who is on vacation, is in charge of processing vouchers.   37.____

38. The activity of the committee at its conferences is always stimulating.   38.____

39. After checking the addresses again, the letters went to the mailroom.   39.____

40. The director, as well as the employees, are interested in sharing the dividends.   40.____

Questions 41-45.

FILING

DIRECTIONS: Each question from 41 through 45 contains four names. For each question, choose the name that should be FIRST if the four names are to be arranged in alphabeti-cal order in accordance with the Rules for Alphabetical Filing given below. Read these rules carefully. Then, for each question, indicate in the space at the right the letter before the name that should be FIRST in alphabet-ical order.

RULES FOR ALPHABETICAL FILING

Names of People

(1) The names of people are filed in strict alphabetical order, first according to the last name, then according to first name or initial, and finally according to middle name or initial. FOR EXAMPLE: George Allen comes before Edward Bell, and Leonard P. Reston comes before Lucille B. Reston.

(2) When last names are the same, FOR EXAMPLE, A. Green and Agnes Green, the one with the initial comes before the one with the name written out when the first initials are identical.

(3) When first and last names are alike and the middle name is given, FOR EXAMPLE, John David Doe and John Devoe Doe, the names should be filed in the alphabetical order of the middle names.

(4) When first and last names are the same, a name without a middle initial comes before one with a middle name or initial. FOR EXAMPLE, John Doe comes before both John A. Doe and John Alan Doe.

(5) When first and last names are the same, a name with a middle initial comes before one with a middle name beginning with the same initial. FOR EXAMPLE: Jack R. Hertz comes before Jack Richard Hertz.

(6) Prefixes such as De, O', Mac, Mc, and Van are filed as written and are treated as part of the names to which they are connected. FOR EXAMPLE: Robert O'Dea is filed before David Olsen.

(7) Abbreviated names are treated as if they were spelled out. FOR EXAMPLE: Chas. is filed as Charles and Thos. is filed as Thomas.

(8) Titles and designations such as Dr., Mr., and Prof, are disregarded in filing.

Names of Organizations

(1) The names of business organizations are filed according to the order in which each word in the name appears. When an organization name bears the name of a person, it is filed according to the rules for filing names of people as given above. FOR EXAMPLE: William Smith Service Co. comes before Television Distributors, Inc.

(2) Where bureau, board, office, or department appears as the first part of the title of a governmental agency, that agency should be filed under the word in the title expressing the chief function of the agency. FOR EXAMPLE: Bureau of the Budget would be filed as if written Budget, (Bureau of the). The Department of Personnel would be filed as if written Personnel, (Department of).

(3) When the following words are part of an organization, they are disregarded: the, of, and.

(4) When there are numbers in a name, they are treated as if they were spelled out. FOR EXAMPLE: 10th Street Bootery is filed as Tenth Street Bootery.

SAMPLE QUESTION:
- A. Jane Earl (2)
- B. James A. Earle (4)
- C. James Earl (1)
- D. J. Earle (3)

The numbers in parentheses show the proper alphabetical order in which these names should be filed. Since the name that should be filed FIRST is James Earl, the answer to the Sample Question is (C).

41.
- A. Majorca Leather Goods
- B. Robert Maiorca and Sons
- C. Maintenance Management Corp.
- D. Majestic Carpet Mills

42.
- A. Municipal Telephone Service
- B. Municipal Reference Library
- C. Municipal Credit Union
- D. Municipal Broadcasting System

43.
- A. Robert B. Pierce
- B. R. Bruce Pierce
- C. Ronald Pierce
- D. Robert Bruce Pierce

44.
- A. Four Seasons Sports Club
- B. 14th. St. Shopping Center
- C. Forty Thieves Restaurant
- D. 42nd St. Theaters

45.
- A. Franco Franceschini
- B. Amos Franchini
- C. Sandra Franceschia
- D. Lilie Franchinesca

Questions 46-50.

SPELLING

DIRECTIONS: In each question, one of the words is misspelled. Select the letter of the misspelled word. *PRINT THE LETTER OF THE CORRECT ANSWER IN THE SPACE AT THE RIGHT.*

46.
- A. option
- B. extradite
- C. comparitive
- D. jealousy

47.
- A. handicaped
- B. assurance
- C. sympathy
- D. speech

48.	A. recommend B. carraige C. disapprove D. independent	48.____
49.	A. ingenuity B. tenet (opinion) C. uncanny D. intrigueing	49.____
50.	A. arduous B. hideous C. iervant D. companies	50.____

KEY (CORRECT ANSWERS)

1. A	11. D	21. A	31. B	41. C
2. B	12. B	22. D	32. B	42. D
3. D	13. D	23. C	33. C	43. B
4. B	14. B	24. A	34. D	44. D
5. D	15. A	25. C	35. C	45. C
6. C	16. B	26. D	36. C	46. C
7. A	17. C	27. D	37. B	47. A
8. C	18. D	28. B	38. D	48. B
9. D	19. A	29. A	39. A	49. D
10. B	20. C	30. C	40. A	50. C'

OFFICE RECORD KEEPING

EXAMINATION SECTION

TEST 1

DIRECTIONS: Each question or incomplete statement is followed by several suggested answers or completions. Select the one that BEST answers the question or completes the statement. *PRINT THE LETTER OF THE CORRECT ANSWER IN THE SPACE AT THE RIGHT.*

Questions 1-5.

DIRECTIONS: Questions 1 through 5 are to be answered on the basis of the following chart to check for address and zip code errors.

    A. No errors
    B. Address only
    C. Zip code only
    D. Both

	Correct List Address	Zip Code	List to be Checked Address	Zip Code	
1.	44-A Western Avenue Bethesda, MD	65564	44-A Western Avenue Bethesda, MD	65654	1.____
2.	567 Opera Lane Jackson, MO	28218	567 Opera Lane Jacksen, MO	28218	2.____
3.	200 W. Jannine Dr. Missoula, MT	30707	200 W. Jannine Dr. Missoula, MT	30307	3.____
4.	28 Champaline Dr. Reno, NV	34101	28 Champaine Way Reno, NV	43101	4.____
5.	65156 Rodojo Parsimony, KY	44590-7326	65156 Rodojo Parsimony, KY	44590-7326	5.____

6. When alphabetized correctly, which of the following would be second?   6.____
    A. flame   B. herring   C. decadence   D. emoticon

7. Which one of the following letters is as far after E as K is before R in the alphabet?   7.____
    A. J   B. K   C. H   D. M

8. How many pairs of the following sets of numbers are exactly alike?   8.____
    134232   123456   432512   561343
    564643   432123   132439   438318

    A. 0   B. 2   C. 3   D. 4

9. When alphabetized correctly, which of the following would be FOURTH?   9.____
   A. microcosm   B. natural   C. lithe   D. nature

10. When alphabetized correctly, which of the following would be THIRD?   10.____
    A. exoskeleton   B. euthanize   C. Europe   D. eurythmic

11. Which one of the following letters is as far before T as S is after I in the alphabet?   11.____
    A. j   B. K   C. M   D. N

12. How many pairs of the following sets of letters are exactly ALIKE?   12.____
    GIHEKE   GIHEKE
    KIWNEB   KWINEB
    PQMZJI   PMQZJI
    OPZIBS   OBZIBS
    PONEHE   POENHE

    A. 0   B. 1   C. 2   D. 4

13. When alphabetized correctly, which of the following would be FIRST?   13.____
    A. Catalina   B. catcher   C. caustic   D. curious

14. Which of the following letters is as far after D as U is after B in the alphabet?   14.____
    A. R   B. V   C. W   D. Z

Questions 15-19.

DIRECTIONS: Use the following information and chart to complete Questions 15 through 19.

Every theft reported to an adjuster needs to be assigned a six-letter code containing the following:

    First Letter: Type of theft
    Second Letter: Witnesses
    Third Letter: Value of stolen item
    Fourth Letter: Location
    Fifth Letter: Time of theft
    Sixth Letter: Elapsed between theft and report

Type of Theft:
A. Breaking and Entering
B. Retail Theft
C. Armed robbery
D. Grand Theft Auto

Witnesses
A. None
B. 1 witness
C. Multiple witnesses
D. Security camera

Location
A. Single Family Home
B. Apartment Building
C. Store
D. Office
E. Vehicle
F. Public Space (Parking Garage, Park, etc.)

Time Elapsed Between Theft and Report
A. 0-1 hour
B. 1-4 hours
C. 4-12 hours
D. 12-24 hours
E. 24 Hours

Time of Theft
A. 7 AM – 1 PM
B. 1 PM – 6 PM
C. 6 PM – 11 PM
D. 11 PM – 3 AM
E. 3 AM – 7 AM

Value of Stolen Items
A. $0-$100
B. $101-$250
C. $251-$500
D. $500-$1000
E. $1001-$5000
F. $5000 or more

15. At 9:30 PM, $175 worth of clothing was stolen from a store. The crime was reported right away by a single store associate. Which of the following would be the CORRECT code?
    A. BCCABB   B. BBBCCA   C. ACCBAB   D. CBCABB

16. A Crossover vehicle worth $4,500 was stolen from a park at approximately 6:45 AM this morning. It was reported stolen at 11:00 AM later that morning by the owner. There were no witnesses. What is the CORRECT code?
    A. DEECAF   B. CFECAE   C. DEFECA   D. DAEFEC

17. Although it was just reported, a breaking and entering occurred 5 days ago at 1:30 AM, according to security cameras that recorded the theft at the accounting firm. Although locks and doors were damaged, nothing was stolen. Which of the following would be the CORRECT code?
    A. ADDEEA   B. ADDDAE   C. ADADDE   D. ADEADE

18. Jill Wagner was held at knifepoint this morning at 11:30 AM when she was walking out of her apartment complex. The thief demanded money, and she gave him $54. She was the only witness and reported the crime immediately. Which of the following would be the CORRECT code?
    A. CBABAA   B. BBABAA   C. CBBABB   D. ABBBCA

19. An artifact worth $5,500 was stolen from the home of Chad Judea this early evening while he was out to dinner from 5:30 PM to 6 PM. When he arrived home at 6 PM, he immediately called the police. There were no witnesses. Which of the following would be the CORRECT code?
    A. AABBAF   B. AABFAF   C. AABABF   D. AAFABA

20. Diatribe means MOST NEARLY
    A. argument   B. cooperation   C. delicate   D. arrogance

21. Vitriolic means MOST NEARLY
    A. flammable   B. fearful   C. spiteful   D. asinine

22. Aplomb means MOST NEARLY
    A. self-righteous   B. respectable   C. dispirited   D. self-confidence

23. Pervicacious means MOST NEARLY
    A. rotten   B. immoral   C. stubborn   D. immortal

24. Detrimental means MOST NEARLY
    A. valuable   B. selfish   C. hopeless   D. harmful

25. Heinous means MOST NEARLY
    A. sweating   B. glorious   C. atrocious   D. moderate

KEY (CORRECT ANSWERS)

1.	C	11.	A
2.	B	12.	B
3.	C	13.	A
4.	D	14.	C
5.	A	15.	B
6.	D	16.	D
7.	B	17.	C
8.	A	18.	A
9.	D	19.	D
10.	B	20.	A

21. C
22. D
23. C
24. D
25. C

TEST 2

DIRECTIONS: Each question or incomplete statement is followed by several suggested answers or completions. Select the one that BEST answers the question or completes the statement. *PRINT THE LETTER OF THE CORRECT ANSWER IN THE SPACE AT THE RIGHT.*

Questions 1-7.

DIRECTIONS: In answering Questions 1 through 7, you will be presented with analogies (known as word relationships). Select the answer choice that BEST completes the analogy.

1. Coordinated is related to movement as speech is related to 1.____
   A. predictive B. rapid C. prophetic D. articulate

2. Pottery is related to shard as wood is related to 2.____
   A. acorn B. chair C. smoke D. kiln

3. Poverty is related to money as famine is related to 3.____
   A. nourishment B. infirmity C. illness D. care

4. Farmland is related to arable as waterway is related to 4.____
   A. impenetrable B. maneuverable
   C. fertile D. deep

5. 19 is related to 17 as 37 is related to 5.____
   A. 39 B. 36 C. 34 D. 31

6. Cup is related to lip as bird is related to 6.____
   A. beak B. grass C. forest D. bush

7. ZRYQ is related to KCJB as PWOV is related to 7.____
   A. GBHA B. ISJT C. ELDK D. EOFP

Questions 8-12.

DIRECTIONS: In answering Questions 8 through 12, each of the questions has a group. Find out which one of the given alternatives will be another member of that group.

8. Springfield, Sacramento, Tallahassee 8.____
   A. Buffalo B. Bangor C. Pittsburgh D. Providence

9. Lock, Shut, Fasten 9.____
   A. Window B. Iron C. Door D. Block

10. Pathology, Radiology, Ophthalmology 10.____
    A. Zoology B. Hematology C. Geology D. Biology

25

11. Karate, Jujitsu, Boxing   11._____
    A. Polo   B. Pole-vault   C. Judo   D. Swimming

12. Newspaper, Hoarding, Television   12._____
    A. Press   B. Rumor   C. Media   D. Broadcast

Questions 13-18.

DIRECTIONS: Questions 13 through 18 are to be answered on the basis of the following pie chart.

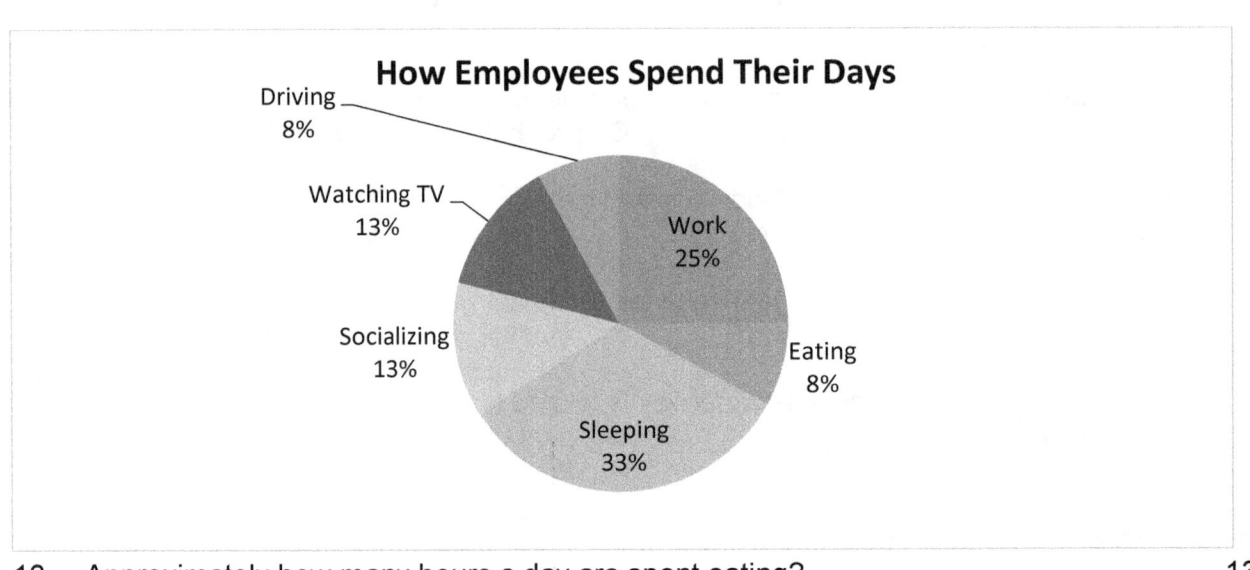

13. Approximately how many hours a day are spent eating?   13._____
    A. 2 hours   B. 5 hours   C. 1 hour   D. 30 minutes

14. According to the graph, for each 48 hour period, about how many hours are   14._____
    spent socializing and watching TV?
    A. 9 hours   B. 6 hours   C. 12 hours   D. 3 hours

15. If an employee ate two-thirds of their meals at a restaurant, what percentage   15._____
    of the total day is spent eating at home?
    A. 2.5%   B. 5.3%   C. 8%   D. 1.4%

16. About how many hours a day are spent working and sleeping?   16._____
    A. 7   B. 10   C. 12   D. 14

17. Which of the following equations could be used to figure out how much time   17._____
    an employee spends watching TV during a week? T equals the total amount of
    time watching TV during the week.
    A. T = 13% x 24 x 7   B. T = 24 x 13 x 7
    C. T = 24/13% x 7   D. T = 1.3 x 7 x 24

18. How many hours a week does the average employee spend socializing?   18._____
    A. 20   B. 22   C. 23   D. 24

Questions 19-25.

DIRECTIONS: Questions 19 through 25 are to be answered on the basis of the following charts.

DIAL DIRECT	WEEKDAY FULL RATE		EVENING 40% DISCOUNT		WEEKEND 60% DISCOUNT	
SAMPLE RATES FROM SEATTLE TO	FIRST MINUTE	EACH ADDITIONAL MINUTE	FIRST MINUTE	EACH ADDITIONAL MINUTE	FIRST MINUTE	EACH ADDITIONAL MINUTE
Savannah, GA	.52	.23	.31	.14	.21	.08
Providence, RI	.52	.223	.31	.14	.21	.08
Golden, CO	.52	.23	.31	.14	.21	.08
Indianapolis, IN	.48	.19	.29	.11	.19	.07
San Diego, CA	.54	.24	.32	.14	.22	.09
Tallahassee, FL	.54	.24	.32	.14	.22	.09
Milwaukee, WI	.57	.27	.34	.16	.23	.09
Minneapolis, MN	.49	.22	.29	.13	.20	.08
Baton Rouge, LA	.52	.23	.31	.14	.21	.08
Buffalo, NY	.52	.23	.31	.14	.21	.08
Annapolis, MD	.54	.24	.32	.14	.22	.09
Washington, DC	.52	.23	.31	.14	.21	.08

OPERATOR ASSISTED		
STATION-TO-STATION		PERSON-TO-PERSON
1 – 10 MILES	$.75	$3.00 FEE FOR ALL MILEAGES
11 - 22 MILES	$1.10	*NOTE: Add to this base charge – the minute rates from the above chart
23-3000 MILES	$1.55	

19. What is the price of a 6-minute dial direct call to Annapolis, MD when you call on a weekend?
    A. $0.59   B. $0.54   C. $0.67   D. $0.49

20. What is the difference in cost between a 10 minute dial direct to Buffalo, NY and a 10 minute person-to-person call to Buffalo, NY?
    A. $1.55   B. $3.00   C. $0.55   D. $4.55

21. What is the price of a 15-minute operator-assisted Station-to-Station call to Indianapolis, IN on a Monday at noon?
    A. $3.74   B. $7.80   C. $3.45   D. $4.69

22. What is the difference in price between an 11-minute dial direct call to Milwaukee, WI at 11:00 AM on a Wednesday and the same call made at 9 PM that night?
    A. $2.27   B. $3.00   C. $1.55   D. $1.336

19.____

20.____

21.____

22.____

23. Which of the following is NOT a type of charge for a dial direct call? 23._____
    A. Holiday   B. Evening   C. Weekend   D. Weekday

24. If a 3.5% tax applied to the total cost of any call, what would be the TOTAL cost of a 13-minute weekday, dial direct call to Golden, CO? 24._____
    A. $3.28   B. $3.39   C. $4.94   D. $6.39

25. What is the amount of discount from a dial direct, weekday call to Tallahassee, FL cost as compared to a dial direct, weekend call to Tallahassee? 25._____
    A. 45%   B. 30%   C. 60%   D. 20%

KEY (CORRECT ANSWERS)

1.	D		11.	C
2.	B		12.	D
3.	A		13.	A
4.	C		14.	C
5.	D		15.	A
6.	A		16.	D
7.	C		17.	A
8.	D		18.	B
9.	D		19.	C
10.	B		20.	B

21. D
22. D
23. A
24. B
25. C

TEST 3

DIRECTIONS: Each question or incomplete statement is followed by several suggested answers or completions. Select the one that BEST answers the question or completes the statement. *PRINT THE LETTER OF THE CORRECT ANSWER IN THE SPACE AT THE RIGHT.*

Questions 1-7.

DIRECTIONS: Questions 1 through 7 are to be answered on the basis of the following graph.

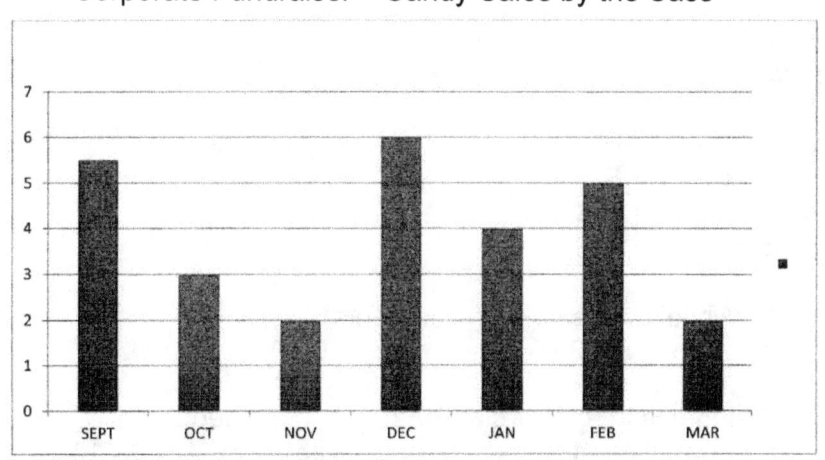

Corporate Fundraiser – Candy Sales by the Case

1. The vertical scale ranging from 0 to 7 represents the number of 1.____
   A. students selling candy
   B. candy sold in each case
   C. days each month that candy was sold
   D. cases of candy sold

2. Which two months had approximately the same amount of candy sold? 2.____
   A. November and March
   B. September and February
   C. November and October
   D. October and March

3. Which month showed a 100% increase in sales over the month of November? 3.____
   A. March   B. January   C. April   D. December

4. From month-to-month, which month saw an approximate 33% drop in sales from the previous month? 4.____
   A. March   B. September   C. January   D. October

5. The amount of candy sold in December is twice the amount of candy sold in which other month? 5.____
   A. October   B. March   C. January   D. September

29

6. What was the total amount of candy sold during the months shown on the graph?
   A. 44 cases   B. 35.5 cases   C. 23.5 cases   D. 27.5 cases

7. If the fundraiser extended the additional five months of the year and added an additional 65% in sales, approximately how many cases would be sold in total for an entire year?
   A. 40.5 cases   B. 37 cases   C. 45 cases   D. 27.5 cases

Questions 8-11.

DIRECTIONS: Questions 8 through 11 are to be answered on the basis of the following chart.

S = 10 students
s = 5 students

Mr. Hucklebee	S S S S s
Ms. Shopenhauer	S S S
Mr. White	S S S s
Mrs. Mulrooney	S S S

8. The size of Mr. White's class is _____ students.
   A. 30   B. 35   C. 40   D. 4

9. The total of all students in all four classes is _____ students.
   A. 150   B. 140   C. 125   D. 14

10. The average class size based on the above chart is _____ students.
    A. 140   B. 45   C. 35   D. 30

11. In order to ensure each teacher has the same amount of students in each class, how many students would need to transfer out of Mr. Hucklebee's class?
    A. 10
    B. 5
    C. 0
    d. 15 would need to transfer into his class

12. When alphabetized correctly, which of the following would be THIRD?
    A. box   B. departed   C. electrical   D. elemental

13. When alphabetized correctly, which of the following would be SECOND?
    A. polarize   B. omnipotent   C. polygraph   D. omniscient

14. When alphabetized correctly, which of the following would be THIRD?
    A. Macklemore, Jonathan   B. Mackelmore, J.
    C. DiCastro, Darian   D. Castro, Darren Henry

15. The group fought through the fog, *shambling* through the night, doing their best to stay upright. 15.____
    The word *shambling* means
    A. frozen in place   B. running
    C. walking awkwardly   D. shivering uncontrollably

16. Many doctors agree that Gen-aspirin is the best for fighting headaches. It comes in different flavors and is easy to swallow. 16.____
    Is this a valid or invalid argument?
    A. Invalid   B. Valid

Questions 17-21.

DIRECTIONS: Questions 17 through 21 are to be answered on the basis of the following paragraph.

Hospital workers and volunteers often ask Mr. Ansley to educate children who are hospitalized with primary ciliary dyskinesia (PCD). As he goes through the precautionary cleaning process (scrubbing, donning sterilized clothes, etc.) in order to see his students, Mr. Ansley wonders why their parents add the stress and pressure of schooling and trying to play catch-up because of the amount of time spent in the hospital and not in the classroom, which is an unfortunate side effect of patients with PCD. These children go through so many painful treatments on a given day that it seems punishing to subject them to schooling as normal children do, especially with life expectancy being as short as it is.

17. What is meant by *precautionary* in the second sentence? 17.____
    A. Careful   B. Protective   C. Sterilizing   D. Medical

18. What is the MAIN idea of this passage? 18.____
    A. The preparation to visit a patient with primary ciliary dyskinesia is extensive.
    B. Children with PCD are unable to live normal lives.
    C. Children with PCD die young.
    D. Certain allowances should be made for children with PCD.

19. What is the author's purpose? 19.____
    A. To advise   B. To educate
    C. To establish credibility D. To amuse

20. What is the author's tone? 20.____
    A. Cruel   B. Sympathetic
    C. Disbelieving   D. Cheerful

21. How is Mr. Ansley so familiar with the procedures used when visiting a child with PCD? 21.____
    A. He has read about it
    B. He works in the hospital.
    C. His child has PCD.
    D. He tutors them on a regular basis.

Questions 22-25.

DIRECTIONS: One of the underlined words in Questions 22 through 25 should be changed. Select the one that should be changed and print the letter of the word that would change the underlined word.

22. After we washed the fruit that had growing in the garden, we knew there was a store that would buy them.
    A. washing   B. grown   C. is   D. No change

23. When the temperature drops under 32 degrees (F), the water on the lake freezes, which allowed children to skate across it.
    A. dropped   B. froze   C. allows   D. No change

24. My friend's bulldog, while chasing cars in the street, always manages to knock over our garbage bins.
    A. chased   B. manage   C. knocks   D. No change

25. Some of the ice on the driveway has melted.
    A. having melted   B. have melted
    C. has melt   D. No change

KEY (CORRECT ANSWERS)

1.	D	11.	A
2.	A	12.	C
3.	B	13.	D
4.	C	14.	B
5.	A	15.	C
6.	D	16.	A
7.	C	17.	C
8.	B	18.	D
9.	B	19.	A
10.	C	20.	B

21. D
22. B
23. C
24. D
25. D

TEST 4

DIRECTIONS: Each question or incomplete statement is followed by several suggested answers or completions. Select the one that BEST answers the question or completes the statement. *PRINT THE LETTER OF THE CORRECT ANSWER IN THE SPACE AT THE RIGHT.*

Questions 1-2.

DIRECTIONS: One of the underlined words in Questions 1 and 2 should be changed. Select the one that should be changed and print the letter of the word that would change the underlined word.

1. You can get to Martha's Vineyard by driving from Boston to Woods Hole. Once there, you can travel over on a boat, but you may find traveling by airplane to be more exciting.
   A. they B. visitors C. it D. No change

   1.____

2. When John wants to go to the store looking for milk and eggs, you must remember to bring his wallet.
   A. them B. he C. its D. No change

   2.____

3. An item that sells for $400 is put on sale at $145. What is the percentage of decrease?
   A. 25% B. 28% C. 64% D. 36%

   3.____

4. Two Junior College Mathematics courses have a total of 510 students. The 9:00 AM class has 60 more than the 12:30 PM class. How many students are in the 12:30 class?
   A. 225 B. 285 C. 255 D. 205

   4.____

5. If a car gets 26 miles per gallon and it has driven 75,210 miles, approximately what is the number of gallons of gas that it has used?
   A. 3,000 B. 2,585 C. 165 D. 1,800

   5.____

6. Which one of the following sentences about proper telephone usage is NOT always correct? When answering a telephone, you should
   A. know who you are speaking to
   B. give the caller your undivided attention
   C. identify yourself to the caller
   D. obtain the information your caller wishes before you do other work

   6.____

7. You are part of the "Safety at Work" committee, which is dedicated to ensuring safety of employees. During your regular shift, you notice an employee in violation of one of your committee's rules. Which of the following actions should you take FIRST?
   A. Speak with the employee about the safety rules and mandate them to stop breaking the rules.
   B. Speak to the employee about safety rules and point out the rule they violated.
   C. Bring up the issue during the next committee meeting.
   D. Report the violation to the employee's superiors.

8. Part of your duties is overseeing employee confidential information. A friend and coworker of yours asks to obtain information concerning another employee. Which is the BEST action to take?
   A. Ask the coworker if you can share the information.
   B. Ask your supervisor if you can give the information to your friend.
   C. Refuse to give the information to your friend.
   D. Give the information to your friend.

9. Which of the following words means the OPPOSITE of protract?
   A. Extend   B. Hesitant   C. Curtail   D. Plethora

10. Which of the following words means the OPPOSITE of conserve?
    A. Relinquish   B. Waste   C. Proficient   D. Rigid

11. Which of the following words means the SAME as dissipate?
    A. Scatter   B. Emancipate
    C. Engage   D. Accumulate

12. Your office just purchased 14 fax machines. Each fax machine costs $79.99. How much did the 14 fax machines cost?
    A. $1,119.86   B. $1,108.77   C. $1,201.44   D. $1,788.22

Questions 13-19.

DIRECTIONS: Questions 13 through 19 are to be answered on the basis of the following chart.

Office City	Sales Rank	Production Materials Produced	Rank for Production	Damaged Materials	Employees	Percent of Profit	Sales Points	Weeks Without Injuries
Springfield	13.6	271	12	1	34	35	36	7
Philadelphia	17	274	4	3	25	41	20	4
Gary	16	260	10	5	34	34	21	3
Boulder	5	10	6	9	38	15	20	8
Miami	81	3	81	77	133	4	2	0
Houston	2	370	2	0	95	66	100	16
Battle Creek	82	290	82	81	91	13	9	2

13. Between Philadelphia and Battle Creek, how many damaged materials were there?
    A. 84   B. 78   C. 45   D. 86

    13.____

14. How many offices have had 5 or more weeks without injuries?
    A. 3   B. 4   C. 2   D. 0

    14.____

15. What was the TOTAL number of damaged materials for the offices in Boulder, Miami, Houston, and Springfield offices?
    A. 91   B. 87   C. 80   D. 77

    15.____

16. What were the TOTAL sales points of Houston, Battle Creek, and Gary?
    A. 115   B. 145   C. 160   D. 130

    16.____

17. Which of the offices had the LOWEST number of weeks without an injury?
    A. Battle Creek   B. Miami   C. Gary   D. Philadelphia

    17.____

18. If worker efficiency is a percentage based on the number of workers at an office and the amount of materials produced, which office has the GREATEST worker efficiency?
    A. Philadelphia   B. Springfield   C. Boulder   D. Gary

    18.____

19. If the company was looking to close a facility, which of the following factors would NOT be a reason to close the Miami office?
    A. Weeks without injury   B. Sales rank
    C. Production materials produced D. Employees

    19.____

Questions 20-25.

DIRECTIONS: In answering Questions 20 through 25, select the sentence in which the underlined word is used correctly.

20. A. Jon needs to increase his capitol by 30% to invest in my business.
    B. The organization is reevaluating it's decision to purchase the building.
    C. The office supply store sells computer paper and stationery.
    D. The quarterback and running back left there helmets on the bus.

    20.____

21. A. The police sergeant sited me for disorderly conduct and driving without a license.
    B. The votes have already been counted.
    C. The professor's theory contradicts the principals of Einstein and Newton.
    D. Who's glass of water is on the table?

    21.____

22. A. The board of trustees decided to accept the CEO's resignation.
    B. Lose hats will help keep your head from hurting.
    C. She complemented me on my exquisite dinner tastes.
    D. Jamaal offered him some sound advise.

    22.____

23. A. In class today, Maya lead us in the reciting of the pledge.
    B. Doctors worry about the affects of drinking red wine right before bed.
    C. The workers used sledge hammers to break up the pavement.
    D. The teacher gave her students wise council.

24. A. This building was formerly the site of one of the city's oldest department stores.
    B. In his position, Albert must be very discrete in handling confidential information.
    C. He was to tired to continue the race.
    D. Each of his mortgage payments as about evenly divided between principle and interest.

25. A. The police spent several hours at the cite of the accident.
    B. A majority of the public support capitol punishment.
    C. The magician used mirrors to create a convincing illusion.
    D. The heiress flouted her wealth by wearing expensive jewelry.

KEY (CORRECT ANSWERS)

1.	D	11.	A
2.	B	12.	A
3.	C	13.	A
4.	A	14.	A
5.	A	15.	B
6.	D	16.	D
7.	B	17.	B
8.	C	18.	A
9.	C	19.	D
10.	B	20.	C

21.	B
22.	A
23.	C
24.	A
25.	C

CLERICAL ABILITIES TEST

Clerical aptitude involves the ability to perceive pertinent detail in verbal or tabular material, to observe differences in copy, to proofread words and numbers, and to avoid perceptual errors in arithmetic computation.

NATURE OF THE TEST

Four types of clerical aptitude questions are presented in the Clerical Abilities Test. There are 120 questions with a short time limit. The test contains 30 questions on name and number checking, 30 on the arrangement of names in correct alphabetical order, 30 on simple arithmetic, and 30 on inspecting groups of letters and numbers. The questions have been arranged in groups or cycles of five questions of each type. The Clerical Abilities Test is primarily a test of speed in carrying out relatively simple clerical tasks. While accuracy on these tasks is important and will be taken into account in the scoring, experience has shown that many persons are so concerned about accuracy that they do the test more slowly than they should. Competitors should be cautioned that speed as well as accuracy is important to achieve a good score.

HOW THE TEST IS ADMINISTERED

Each competitor should be given a copy of the test booklet with sample questions on the cover page, an answer sheet, and a medium No. 2 pencil. Ten minutes are allowed to study the directions and sample questions and to answer the questions in the proper boxes on the two pages.
The separate answer sheet should be used for the test proper. Fifteen minutes are allowed for the test.

HOW THE TEST IS SCORED

The correct answers should be counted and recorded. The number of incorrect answers must also be counted because one-fourth of the number of incorrect answers is subtracted from the number of right answers. An omission is considered as neither a right nor a wrong answer. The score on this test is the number of right answers minus one-fourth of the number of wrong answers (fractions of one-half or less are dropped). For example, if an applicant had answered 89 questions correctly and 10 questions incorrectly, and had omitted 1 question, his score would be 87.

EXAMINATION SECTION

DIRECTIONS: This test contains four kinds of questions. There are some of each kind on each page in the booklet. The time limit for the test will be announced by the examiner.
Use the special pencil furnished by the examiner in marking your answers on the separate answer sheet. For each question, there are five suggested answers. Decide which answer is correct, find the number of the question on the answer sheet, and make a solid black mark between the dotted lines just below the letter of your answer. If you wish to change your answer, erase the first mark completely, do not merely cross it out.

SAMPLE QUESTIONS

In each line across the page there are three names or numbers that are much alike. Compare the three names or numbers and decide which ones are exactly alike. On the Sample Answer Sheet at the right, mark the answer

- A. if ALL THREE names or numbers are exactly ALIKE
- B. if only the FIRST and SECOND names or numbers are exactly ALIKE
- C. if only the FIRST and THIRD names or numbers are exactly ALIKE
- D. if only the SECOND and THIRD names or numbers are exactly ALIKE
- E. if ALL THREE names or numbers are DIFFERENT

I.	Davis Hazen	David Hozen	David Hazen
II.	Lois Appel	Lois Appel	Lois Apfel
III.	June Allan	Jane Allan	Jane Allan
IV.	10235	10235	10235
V.	32614	32164	32614

It will be to your advantage to learn what A, B, C, D, and E stand for. If you finish the sample questions before you are told to turn to the test, study them.

In the next group of sample questions, there is a name in a box at the left, and four other names in alphabetical order at the right. Find the correct space for the boxed name so that it will be in alphabetical order with the others, and mark the letter of that space as your answer.

VI. [Jones, Jane]

A. →
   Goodyear, G.L.
B. →
   Haddon, Harry
C. →
   Jackson, Mary
D. →
   Jenkins, William
E. →

VII. [Kessler, Neilson]

A. →
   Kessel, Carl
B. →
   Kessinger, D.J.
C. →
   Kessler, Karl
D. →
   Kessner, Lewis
E. →

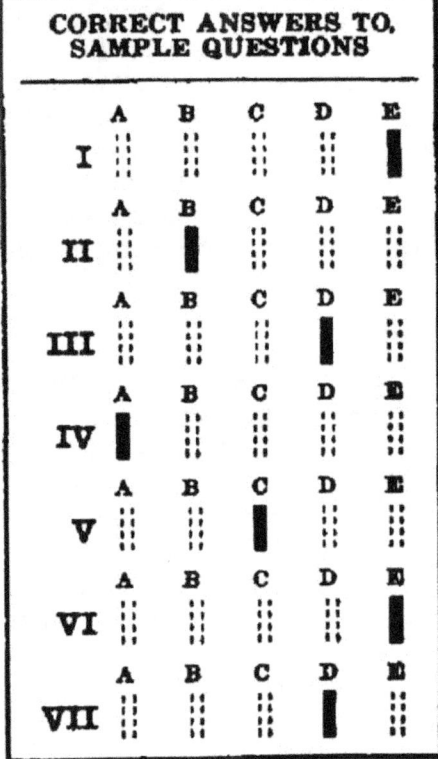

DIRECTIONS: In the following questions, complete the equation and find your answer among the list of suggested answers. Mark the Sample Answer Sheet A, B, C, or D for the answer you obtained; or if your answer is not among these, mark E for that question.

VIII. Add: 22
             +33

A. 44   B. 45   C. 54   D. 55   E. None of these

IX. Subtract: 24
              - 3

A. 20   B. 21   C. 27   D. 29   E. None of these

X. Multiply: 25
              x 5

A. 100   B. 115   C. 125   D. 135   E. None of these

40

XI. Divide: 6/126̄

    A. 20   B. 22   C. 24   D. 26   E. None of these

DIRECTIONS: There is one set of suggested answers for the next group of sample questions. Do not try to memorize these answers, because there will be a different set on each age in the test.

To find the answer to a question, find which suggested answer contains numbers and letters, all of which appear in the question. If no suggested answer fits, mark E for that question.

XII. 8 N K 9 G T 4 6

XIII. T 9 7 Z 6 L 3 K

XIV. Z 7 G K 3 9 8 N

XV. 3 K 9 4 6 G Z L

XVI. Z N 7 3 8 K T 9

Suggested Answers
A = 7, 9, G, K
B = 8, 9, T, Z
C = 6, 7, K, Z
D = 6, 8, G, T
E = None of the above

After you have marked your answers to all the questions on the Sample Answer Sheets on this page and on the front page of the booklet, check them with the answers in the boxes marked Correct Answers To Sample Questions.

Questions 1-5.

In Questions 1 through 5, compare the three names or numbers, and mark
    A. if ALL THREE names or numbers are exactly ALIKE
    B. if only the FIRST and SECOND names or numbers are exactly ALIKE
    C. if only the FIRST and THIRD names or numbers are exactly ALIKE
    D. if only the SECOND and THIRD names or numbers are exactly ALIKE
    E. if ALL THREE names or numbers are DIFFERENT

1.	5261383	5261383	5261338
2.	8125690	8126690	8125609
3.	W.E. Johnston	W.E. Johnson	W.E. Johnson
4.	Vergil L. Muller	Vergil L. Muller	Vergil L. Muller

5.   Atherton R. Warde   Asheton R. Warde   Atherton P. Warde

Questions 6-10.

In Questions 6 through 10, find the correct place for the name in the box

6. | Hackett, Gerald |

   A. →
      Habert, James
   B. →
      Hachett, J.J.
   C. →
      Hachetts, K. Larson
   D. →
      Hachettson, Leroy
   E. →

7. | Margenroth, Alvin |

   A. →
      Margeroth, Albert
   B. →
      Margestein, Dan
   C. →
      Margestein, David
   D. →
      Margue, Edgar
   E. →

8. | Bobbitt, Olivier E. |

   A. →
      Bobbitt, D. Olivier
   B. →
      Bobbitt, Olivia B
   C. →
      Bobbitt, Olivia H.
   D. →
      Bobbitt, R. Olivia
   E. →

9. | Mosley, Werner |

   A. →
      Mosely, Albert J.
   B. →
      Mosley, Alvin
   C. →
      Mosley, S.M.
   D. →
      Mozley, Vinson N.
   E. →

10. Youmuns, Frank L.

   A. → Youmons, Frank G.
   B. → Youmons, Frank H.
   C. → Youmons, Frank K.
   D. → Youmons, Frank M.
   E. →

Questions 11-15.

11. Add: 43
       +32

   A. 55   B. 65   C. 66   D. 75   E. None of these

12. Subtract: 83
            - 4

   A. 73   B. 79   C. 80   D. 89   E. None of these

13. Multiply: 41
            x 7

   A. 281   B. 287   C. 291   D. 297   E. None of these

14. Divide: 6/306

   A. 44   B. 51   C. 52   D. 60   E. None of these

15. Add: 37
       +15

   A. 42   B. 52   C. 53   D. 62   E. None of these

Questions 16-20.

In Questions 16 through 20, find which one of the suggested answers appears in that question.

16. 6 2 5 K 4 P T G

17. L 4 7 2 T 6 V K

18. 3 5 4 L 9 V T G

19. G 4 K 7 L 3 5 Z

SUGGESTED ANSWERS
A = 4, 5, K, T
B = 4, 7, G, K
C = 2, 5, G, L
D = 2, 7, L, T
E = None of the above

20. 4 K 2 9 N 5 T G

Questions 21-25.

In Questions 21 through 25, compare the three names or numbers, and mark
    A. if ALL THREE names or numbers are exactly ALIKE
    B. if only the FIRST and SECOND names or numbers are exactly ALIKE
    C. if only the FIRST and THIRD names or numbers are exactly ALIKE
    D. if only the SECOND and THIRD names or numbers are exactly ALIKE
    E. if ALL THREE names or numbers are DIFFERENT

21. 2395890   2395890   2395890

22. 1926341   1926347   1926314

23. E. Owens McVey   E. Owen McVey   E. Owen McVay

24. Emily Neal Rouse   Emily Neal Rowse   Emily Neal Rowse

25. H. Merritt Audubon   H. Merriott Audubon   H. Merritt Audubon

Questions 26-30.

In Questions 26 through 30, find the correct place for the name in the box.

26. | Watters, N.O. |

A. →
Waters, Charles L.
B. →
Waterson, Nina P.
C. →
Watson, Nora J.
D. →
Wattwood, Paul A.
E. →

27. | Johnston, Edward |

A. →
Johnston, Edgar R.
B. →
Johnston, Edmond
C. →
Johnston, Edmund
D. →
Johnstone, Edmund A.
E. →

28. | Rensch, Adeline |

A. →
Ramsay, Amos
B. →
Remschel, Augusta
C. →
Renshaw, Austin
D. →
Rentzel, Becky
E. →

29. | Schnyder, Maurice |

A. →
Schneider, Martin
B. →
Schneider, Mertens
C. →
Schnyder, Newman
D. →
Schreibner, Norman
E. →

30. | Freedenburg, C. Erma |

A. →
Freedenberg, Emerson
B. →
Freedenberg, Erma
C. →
Freedenberg, Erma E.
D. →
Freedinberg, Erma F.
E. →

Questions 31-35.

31. Subtract: 68
     - 47

    A. 10   B. 11   C. 20   D. 22   E. None of these

32. Multiply: 50
     x 8

    A. 400   B. 408   C. 450   D. 458   E. None of these

33. Divide: 9/180

    A. 20   B. 29   C. 30   D. 39   E. None of these

34. Add: 78
     + 63

    A. 131   B. 140   C. 141   D. 151   E. None of these

35. Add: 89
    -70

   A. 9   B. 18   C. 19   D. 29   E. None of these

Questions 36-40.

In Questions 36 through 40, find which one of the suggested answers appears in that question.

36. 9 G Z 3 L 4 6 N

37. L 5 N K 4 3 9 V

38. 8 2 V P 9 L Z 5

39. V P 9 Z 5 L 8 7

40. 5 T 8 N 2 9 V L

SUGGESTED ANSWERS
A = 4, 9, L, V
B = 4, 5, N, Z
C = 5, 8, L, Z
D = 8, 9, N, V
E = None of the above

Questions 41-45.

In Questions 41 through 45, compare the three names or numbers, and mark
   A. if ALL THREE names or numbers are exactly ALIKE
   B. if only the FIRST and SECOND names or numbers are exactly ALIKE
   C. if only the FIRST and THIRD names or numbers are exactly ALIKE
   D. if only the SECOND and THIRD names or numbers are exactly ALIKE
   E. if ALL THREE names or numbers are DIFFERENT

41.	6219354	621354	6219354
42.	2312793	2312793	2312793
43.	1065407	1065407	1065047
44.	Francis Ransdell	Frances Ramsdell	Francis Ramsdell
45.	Cornelius Detwiler	Cornelius Detwiler	Cornelius Detwiler

Questions 46-50.

In Questions 46 through 50, find the correct place for the name in the box.

46. DeMattia, Jessica

A. →
DeLong, Jesse
B. →
DeMatteo, Jessie
C. →
Derby, Jessie S.
D. →
DeShazo, L.M.
E. →

47. Theriault, Louis

A. →
Therien, Annette
B. →
Therien, Elaine
C. →
Thibeault, Gerald
D. →
Thiebeault, Pierre
E. →

48. Gaston, M. Hubert

A. →
Gaston, Dorothy M.
B. →
Gaston, Henry N.
C. →
Gaston, Isabel
D. →
Gaston, M. Melvin
E. →

49. SanMiguel, Carlos

A. →
SanLuis, Juana
B. →
Santilli, Laura
C. →
Stinnett, Nellie
D. →
Stoddard, Victor
E. →

50. | DeLaTour, Hall F. | A. →
                              DeLargy, Harold
                           B. →
                              DeLathouder, Hilda
                           C. →
                              Lathrop, Hillary
                           D. →
                              LaTour, Hulbert E.
                           E. →

Questions 51-55.

51. Multiply: 62
             x 5

    A. 300   B. 310   C. 315   D. 360   E. None of these

52. Divide: 3/153

    A. 41   B. 43   C. 51   D. 53   E. None of these

53. Add: 47
        +21

    A. 58   B. 59   C. 67   D. 68   E. None of these

54. Subtract: 87
             - 42

    A. 34   B. 35   C. 44   D. 45   E. None of these

55. Multiply: 37
             x 3

    A. 91   B. 101   C. 104   D. 114   E. None of these

Questions 56-60.

For Questions 56 through 60, find which one of the suggested answers appears in that question.

56. N 5 4 7 T K 3 Z

57. 8 5 3 V L 2 Z N

58. 7 2 5 N 9 K L V

59. 9 8 L 2 5 Z K V

60. Z 6 5 V 9 3 P N

SUGGESTED ANSWERS
A = 3, 8, K, N
B = 5, 8, N, V
C = 3, 9, V, Z
D = 5, 9, K, Z
E = None of the above

Questions 61-65.

In Questions 61 through 65, compare the three names or numbers, and mark
  A. if ALL THREE names or numbers are exactly ALIKE
  B. if only the FIRST and SECOND names or numbers are exactly ALIKE
  C. if only the FIRST and THIRD names or numbers are exactly ALIKE
  D. if only the SECOND and THIRD names or numbers are exactly ALIKE
  E. if ALL THREE names or numbers are DIFFERENT

61. 6452054   6452654   6452054

62. 8501268   8501268   8501286

63. Ella Burk Newham Ella Burk Newnham Elena Burk Newnham

64. Jno. K. Ravencroft Jno. H. Ravencroft Jno. H. Ravencoft

65. Martin Wills Pullen Martin Wills Pulen Martin Wills Pullen

Questions 66-70.

In Questions 66 through 70, find the correct place for the name in the box.

66. O'Bannon, M.J.
    A. →
       O'Beirne, B.B.
    B. →
       Oberlin, E.L.
    C. →
       Oberneir, L.P.
    D. →
       O'Brian, S.F.
    E. →

67. Entsminger, Jacob
    A. →
       Ensminger, J.
    B. →
       Entsminger, J.A.
    C. →
       Entsminger, Jack
    D. →
       Entsminger, James
    E. →

68. | Iacone, Pete R. |
   A. →
      Iacone, Pedro
   B. →
      Iacone, Pedro M.
   C. →
      Iacone, Peter F.
   D. →
      Iascone, Peter W.
   E. →

69. | Sheppard, Gladys |
   A. →
      Shepard, Dwight
   B. →
      Shepard, F.H.
   C. →
      Shephard, Louise
   D. →
      Shepperd, Stella
   E. →

70. | Thackton, Melvin T. |
   A. →
      Thackston, Milton G.
   B. →
      Thackston, Milton W.
   C. →
      Thackston, Theodore
   D. →
      Thackston, Thomas G.
   E. →

Questions 71-75.

71. Divide: $7\overline{)357}$

    A. 51   B. 52   C. 53   D. 54   E. None of these

72. Add: 58
         +27

    A. 75   B. 84   C. 85   D. 95   E. None of these

73. Subtract: 86
            - 57

    A. 18   B. 29   C. 38   D. 39   E. None of these

74. Multiply: 68
    x 4

    A. 242 B. 264 C. 272 D. 274 E. None of these

75. Divide: 9/639

    A. 71 B. 73 C. 81 D. 83 E. None of these

Questions 76-80.

For Questions 76 through 80, find which one of the suggested answers appears in that question.

76. 6 Z T N 8 7 4 V

77. V 7 8 6 N 5 P L

78. N 7 P V 8 4 2 L

79. 7 8 G 4 3 V L T

80. 4 8 G 2 T N 6 L

SUGGESTED ANSWERS
A = 2, 7, L, N
B = 2, 8, T, V
C = 6, 8, L, T
D = 6, 7, N, V
E = None of the above

Questions 81-85.

In Questions 81 through 85, compare the three names or numbers, and mark
    A. if ALL THREE names or numbers are exactly ALIKE
    B. if only the FIRST and SECOND names or numbers are exactly ALIKE
    C. if only the FIRST and THIRD names or numbers are exactly ALIKE
    D. if only the SECOND and THIRD names or numbers are exactly ALIKE
    E. if ALL THREE names or numbers are DIFFERENT

81. 3457988	3457986	3457986
82. 4695682	4695862	4695682
83. Stricklund Kanedy	Stricklund Kanedy	Stricklund Kanedy
84. Joy Harbor Witner	Joy Harloe Witner	Joy Harloe Witner
85. R.M.O. Uberroth	R.M.O. Uberroth	R.N.O. Uberroth

Questions 86-90.

In Questions 86 through 90, find the correct place for the name in the box.

86. | Dunlavey, M. Hilary |

A. →
Dunleavy, Hilary G.
B. →
Dunleavy, Hilary K.
C. →
Dunleavy, Hilary S.
D. →
Dunleavy, Hilery W.
E. →

87. | Yarbrough, Maria |

A. →
Yabroudy, Margy
B. →
Yarboro, Marie
C. →
Yarborough, Marina
D. →
Yarborough, Mary
E. →

88. | Prouty, Martha |

A. →
Proutey, Margaret
B. →
Proutey, Maude
C. →
Prouty, Myra
D. →
Prouty, Naomi
E. →

89. | Pawlowicz, Ruth M. |

A. →
Pawalek, Edward
B. →
Pawelek, Flora G.
C. →
Pawlowski, Joan M.
D. →
Pawtowski, Wanda
E. →

90. | Vanstory, George |

A. →
   Vanover, Eva
B. →
   VanSwinderen, Floyd
C. →
   VanSyckle, Harry
D. →
   Vanture, Laurence
E. →

Questions 91-95

91. Add: 28
         +35

   A. 53   B. 62   C. 64   D. 73   E. None of these

92. Subtract: 78
              -69

   A. 7   B. 8   C. 18   D. 19   E. None of these

93. Multiply: 86
              x 6

   A. 492   B. 506   C. 516   D. 526   E. None of these

94. Divide: 8/648

   A. 71   B. 76   C. 81   D. 89   E. None of these

95. Add: 97
         +34

   A. 131   B. 132   C. 140   D. 141   E. None of these

Questions 96-100.

For Questions 96 through 100, find which one of the suggested answers appears in that question.

96. V 5 7 Z N 9 4 T

97. 4 6 P T 2 N K 9

98. 6 4 N 2 P 8 Z K

99. 7 P 5 2 4 N K T

100. K T 8 5 4 N 2 P

SUGGESTED ANSWERS
A = 2, 5, N, Z
B = 4, 5, N, P
C = 2, 9, P, T
D = 4, 9, T, Z
E = None of the above

Questions 101-105.

In Questions 101 through 105, compare the three names or numbers, and mark
A. if ALL THREE names or numbers are exactly ALIKE
B. if only the FIRST and SECOND names or numbers are exactly ALIKE
C. if only the FIRST and THIRD names or numbers are exactly ALIKE
D. if only the SECOND and THIRD names or numbers are exactly ALIKE
E. if ALL THREE names or numbers are DIFFERENT

101. 1592514   1592574   1592574

102. 2010202   2010202   2010220

103. 6177396   6177936   6177396

104. Drusilla S. Ridgeley   Drusilla S. Ridgeley   Drusilla S. Ridgeley

105. Andrei I. Toumantzev   Andrei I. Tourmantzev   Andrei I. Toumantzov

Questions 106-110.

In Questions 106 through 110, find the correct place for the name in the box.

106. | Fitzsimmons, Hugh |

A. →
Fitts, Harold
B. →
Fitzgerald, June
C. →
FitzGibbon, Junius
D. →
FitzSimons, Martin
E. →

107. | D'Amato, Vincent |

A. →
Daly, Steven
B. →
D'Amboise, S. Vincent
C. →
Daniel, Vail
D. →
DeAlba, Valentina
E. →

108. Schaeffer, Roger D.

A. →
   Schaffert, Evelyn M.
B. →
   Schaffner, Margaret M.
C. →
   Schafhirt, Milton G.
D. →
   Shafer, Richard E.
E. →

109. White-Lewis, Cecil

A. →
   Whitelaw, Cordelia
B. →
   White-Leigh, Nancy
C. →
   Whitely, Rodney
D. →
   Whitlock, Warren
E. →

110. VanDerHeggen, Don

A. →
   VanDemark, Doris
B. →
   Vandenberg, H.E.
C. →
   VanDercook, Marie
D. →
   vanderLinden, Robert
E. →

Questions 111-115.

111. Add: 75
         +49

   A. 124   B. 125   C. 134   D. 225   E. None of these

112. Subtract: 69
              - 45

   A. 14   B. 23   C. 24   D. 26   E. None of these

113. Multiply: 36
              x 8

   A. 246   B. 262   C. 288   D. 368   E. None of these

114. Divide: 8/̄3̄2̄8̄

   A. 31   B. 41   C. 42   D. 48   E. None of these

115. Multiply: 58
              x 9

   A. 472   B. 513   C. 521   D. 522   E. None of these

Questions 116-120.

For Questions 116 through 120, find which one of the suggested answers appears in that question.

116. Z 3 N P G 5 4 2

117. 6 N 2 8 G 4 P T

118. 6 N 4 T V G 8 2

119. T 3 P 4 N 8 G 2

120. 6 7 K G N 2 L 5

SUGGESTED ANSWERS:
A = 2, 3, G, N
B = 2, 6, N, T
C = 3, 4, G, K
D = 4, 6, K, T
E = None of the above

KEY (CORRECT ANSWERS)

1. B	21. A	41. A	61. C	81. D	101. D
2. E	22. E	42. A	62. B	82. C	102. B
3. D	23. E	43. B	63. E	83. A	103. C
4. A	24. D	44. E	64. E	84. D	104. A
5. E	25. C	45. A	65. C	85. B	105. E
6. E	26. D	46. C	66. A	86. A	106. D
7. A	27. D	47. A	667. D	87. E	107. B
8. D	28. C	48. D	68. C	88. C	108. A
9. B	29. C	49. B	69. D	89. C	109. C
10. E	30. D	50. C	70. E	90. B	110. D
11. D	31. E	51. B	71. A	91. E	111. A
12. B	32. A	52. C	72. C	92. E	112. C
13. B	33. A	53. D	73. B	93. C	113. C
14. B	34. C	54. D	74. C	94. C	114. B
15. B	35. C	55. E	75. A	95. A	115. D
16. A	36. E	56. E	76. D	96. D	116. A
17. D	37. A	57. B	77. D	97. C	117. B
18. E	38. C	58. E	78. A	98. E	118. B
19. B	39. C	59. D	79. E	99. B	119. A
20. A	40. D	60. C	80. C	100. B	120. E

CLERICAL ABILITIES
EXAMINATION SECTION
TEST 1

DIRECTIONS: Each question or incomplete statement is followed by several suggested answers or completions. Select the one that BEST answers the question or completes the statement. *PRINT THE LETTER OF THE CORRECT ANSWER IN THE SPACE AT THE RIGHT.*

Questions 1-4.

DIRECTIONS: Questions 1 through 4 are to be answered on the basis of the information given below.

    The most commonly used filing system and the one that is easiest to learn is alphabetical filing. This involves putting records in an A to Z order, according to the letters of the alphabet. The name of a person is filed by using the following order: first, the surname or last name; second, the first name; third, the middle name or middle initial. For example, *Henry C. Young* is filed under *Y* and thereafter under *Young, Henry C.* The name of a company is filed in the same way. For example, *Long Cabinet Co.* is filed under *L* while *John T. Long Cabinet Co.* is filed under *L* and thereafter under *Long, John T. Cabinet Co.*

1. The one of the following which lists the names of persons in the CORRECT alphabetical order is:
   A. Mary Carrie, Helen Carrol, James Carson, John Carter
   B. James Carson, Mary Carrie, John Carter, Helen Carrol
   C. Helen Carrol, James Carson, John Carter, Mary Carrie
   D. John Carter, Helen Carrol, Mary Carrie, James Carson

2. The one of the following which lists the names of persons in the CORRECT alphabetical order is:
   A. Jones, John C.; Jones, John A.; Jones, John P.; Jones, John K.
   B. Jones, John P.; Jones, John K.; Jones, John C.; Jones, John A.
   C. Jones, John A.; Jones, John C.; Jones, John K.; Jones, John P.
   D. Jones, John K.; Jones, John C.; Jones, John A.; Jones, John P.

3. The one of the following which lists the names of the companies in the CORRECT alphabetical order is:
   A. Blane Co., Blake Co., Block Co., Blear Co.
   B. Blake Co., Blane Co., Blear Co., Block Co.
   C. Block Co., Blear Co., Blane Co., Blake Co.
   D. Blear Co., Blake Co., Blane Co., Block Co.

1.____

2.____

3.____

4. You are to return to the file an index card on *Barry C. Wayne Materials and Supplies Co.*
Of the following, the CORRECT alphabetical group that you should return the index card to is
  A. A to G
  B. H to M
  C. N to S
  D. T to Z

Questions 5-10.

DIRECTIONS: In each of Questions 5 through 10, the names of four people are given. For each question, choose as your answer the one of the four names given which should be filed FIRST according to the usual system of alphabetical filing of names, as described in the following paragraph.

In filing names, you must start with the last name. Names are filed in order of the first letter of the last name, then the second letter, etc. Therefore, BAILY would be filed before BROWN, which would be filed before COLT. A name with fewer letters of the same type comes first, i.e., Smith before Smithe. If the last names are the same, the names are filed alphabetically by the first name. If the first name is an initial, a name with an initial would come before a first name that starts with the same letter as the initial. Therefore, I. BROWN would come before IRA BROWN. Finally, if both last name and first name are the same, the name would be filed alphabetically by the middle name, once again an initial coming before a middle name which starts with the same letter as the initial. If there is no middle name at all, the name would come before those with middle initials or names.

SAMPLE QUESTION:
  A. Lester Daniels
  B. William Dancer
  C. Nathan Danzig
  D. Dan Lester

The last names beginning with D are filed before the last name beginning with L. Since DANIELS, DANCER, and DANZIG all begin with the same three letters, you must look at the fourth letter of the last name to determine which name should be filed first. C comes before I or Z in the alphabet, so DANCER is filed before DANIELS or DANZIG. Therefore, the answer to the above sample question is B.

5. A. Scott Biala
   B. Mary Byala
   C. Martin Baylor
   D. Francis Bauer

6. A. Howard J. Black
   B. Howard Black
   C. J. Howard Black
   D. John H. Black

7. A. Theodora Garth Kingston
   B. Theadore Barth Kingston
   C. Thomas Kingston
   D. Thomas T. Kingston

8. A. Paulette Mary Huerta
    B. Paul M. Huerta
    C. Paulette L. Huerta
    D. Peter A. Huerta

9. A. Martha Hunt Morgan
    B. Martin Hunt Morgan
    C. Mary H. Morgan
    D. Martine H. Morgan

10. A. James T. Meerschaum
    B. James M. Mershum
    C. James F. Mearshaum
    D. James N. Meshum

Questions 11-14.

DIRECTIONS: Questions 11 through 14 are to be answered SOLELY on the basis of the following information.

You are required to file various documents in file drawers which are labeled according to the following pattern:

DOCUMENTS

MEMOS		LETTERS	
File	Subject	File	Subject
84PM1	(A-L)	84PC1	(A-L)
84PM2	(M-Z)	84PC2	(M-Z)

REPORTS		INQUIRIES	
File	Subject	File	Subject
84PR1	(A-L)	84PQ1	(A-L)
84PR2	(M-Z)	84PQ2	(M-Z)

11. A letter dealing with a burglary should be filed in the drawer labeled
    A. 84PM1   B. 84PC1   C. 84PR1   D. 84PQ2

12. A report on Statistics should be found in the drawer labeled
    A. 84PM1   B. 84PC2   C. 84PR2   D. 84PQS

13. An inquiry is received about parade permit procedures. It should be filed in the drawer labeled
    A. 84PM2   B. 84PC1   C. 84PR1   D. 84PQ2

14. A police officer has a question about a robbery report you filed. You should pull this file from the drawer labeled
    A. 84PM1   B. 84PM2   C. 84PR1   D. 84PR2

Questions 15-22.

DIRECTIONS: Each of Questions 15 through 22 consists of four or six numbered names. For each question, choose the option (A, B, C, or D) which indicates the order in which the names should be filed in accordance with the following filing instructions:
- File alphabetically according to last name, then first name, then middle initial.
- File according to each successive letter within a name.
- When comparing two names in which the letters in the longer name are identical to the corresponding letters in the shorter name, the shorter name is filed first.
- When the last names are the same, initials are always filed before names beginning with the same letter.

15. I. Ralph Robinson
    II. Alfred Ross
    III. Luis Robles
    IV. James Roberts

    The CORRECT filing sequence for the above names should be
    A. IV, II, I, III   B. I, IV, III, II   C. III, IV, I, II   D. IV, I, III, II

16. I. Irwin Goodwin
    II. Inez Gonzalez
    III. Irene Goodman
    IV. Ira S. Goodwin
    V. Ruth I. Goldstein
    VI. M.B. Goodman

    The CORRECT filing sequence for the above names should be
    A. V, II, I, IV, III, VI
    B. V, II, VI, III, IV, I
    C. V, II, III, VI, IV, I
    D. V, II, III, VI, I, IV

17. I. George Allan
    II. Gregory Allen
    III. Gary Allen
    IV. George Allen

    The CORRECT filing sequence for the above names should be
    A. IV, III, I, II   B. I, IV, II, III   C. III, IV, I, II   D. I, III, IV, II

18. I. Simon Kauffman
    II. Leo Kaufman
    III. Robert Kaufmann
    IV. Paul Kauffmann

    The CORRECT filing sequence for the above names should be
    A. I, IV, II, III   B. II, IV, III, I   C. III, II, IV, I   D. I, II, III, IV

19. I. Roberta Williams
    II. Robin Wilson
    III. Roberta Wilson
    IV. Robin Williams

    The CORRECT filing sequence for the above names should be
    A. III, II, IV, I   B. I, IV, III, II   C. I, II, III, IV   D. III, I, II, IV

20. I. Lawrence Shultz
    II. Albert Schultz
    III. Theodore Schwartz
    IV. Thomas Schwarz
    V. Alvin Schultz
    VI. Leonard Shultz

    The CORRECT filing sequence for the above names should be
    A. II, V, III, IV, I, VI
    B. IV, III, V, I, II, VI
    C. II, V, I, VI, III, IV
    D. I, VI, II, V, III, IV

21. I. McArdle
    II. Mayer
    III. Maletz
    IV. McNiff
    V. Meyer
    VI. MacMahon

    The CORRECT filing sequence for the above names should be
    A. I, IV, VI, III, II, V
    B. II, I, IV, VI, III, V
    C. VI, III, II, I, IV, V
    D. VI, III, II, V, I, IV

22. I. Jack E. Johnson
    II. R.H. Jackson
    III. Bertha Jackson
    IV. J.T. Johnson
    V. Ann Johns
    VI. John Jacobs

    The CORRECT filing sequence for the above names should be
    A. II, III, VI, V, IV, I
    B. III, II, VI, V, IV, I
    C. VI, II, III, I, V, IV
    D. III, II, VI, IV, V, I

Questions 23-30.

DIRECTIONS: The code table below shows 10 letters with matching numbers. For each question, there are three sets of letters. Each set of letters is followed by a set of numbers which may or may not match their correct letter according to the code table. For each question, check all three sets of letters and numbers and mark your answer:
    A. if no pairs are correctly matched
    B. if only one pair is correctly matched
    C. if only two pairs are correctly matched
    D. if all three pairs are correctly matched

CODE TABLE

T	M	V	D	S	P	R	G	B	H
1	2	3	4	5	6	7	8	9	0

SAMPLE QUESTION: TMVDSP – 123456
                                  RGBHTM – 789011
                                  DSPRGB – 256789

In the sample question above, the first set of numbers correctly match its set of letters. But the second and third pairs contain mistakes. In the second pair, M is correctly matched with number 1. According to the code table, letter M should be correctly matched with number 2. In the third pair, the letter D is incorrectly matched with number 2. According to the code table, letter D should be correctly matched with number 4. Since only one of the pairs is correctly matched, the answer to this sample question is B.

23. RSBMRM – 759262
    GDSRVH – 845730
    VDBRTM - 349713

24. TGVSDR – 183247
    SMHRDP – 520647
    TRMHSR - 172057

25. DSPRGM – 456782
    MVDBHT – 234902
    HPMDBT - 062491

26. BVPTRD – 936184
    GDPHMB – 807029
    GMRHMV – 827032

27. MGVRSH – 283750
    TRDMBS – 174295
    SPRMGV - 567283

23._____

24._____

25._____

26._____

27._____

28. SGBSDM – 489542   28.____
    MGHPTM – 290612
    MPBMHT - 269301

29. TDPBHM – 146902   29.____
    VPBMRS – 369275
    GDMBHM - 842902

30. MVPTBV – 236194   30.____
    PDRTMB – 47128
    BGTMSM - 981232

KEY (CORRECT ANSWERS)

1.	A	11.	B	21.	C
2.	C	12.	C	22.	B
3.	B	13.	D	23.	B
4.	D	14.	D	24.	B
5.	D	15.	D	25.	C
6.	B	16.	C	26.	A
7.	B	17.	D	27.	D
8.	B	18.	A	28.	A
9.	A	19.	B	29.	D
10.	C	20.	A	30.	A

TEST 2

DIRECTIONS: Each question or incomplete statement is followed by several suggested answers or completions. Select the one that BEST answers the question or completes the statement. *PRINT THE LETTER OF THE CORRECT ANSWER IN THE SPACE AT THE RIGHT.*

Questions 1-10.

DIRECTIONS: Questions 1 through 10 each consists of two columns, each containing four lines of names, numbers and/or addresses. For each question, compare the lines in Column I with the lines in Column II to see if they match exactly, and mark your answer A, B, C, or D, according to the following instructions:
    A. all four lines match exactly
    B. only three lines match exactly
    C. only two lines match exactly
    D. only one line matches exactly

    COLUMN I   COLUMN II

1.   I.   Earl Hodgson   Earl Hodgson   1.____
   II. 1409870   1408970
   III. Shore Ave.   Schore Ave.
   IV. Macon Rd.   Macon Rd.

2.   I.   9671485   9671485   2.____
   II. 470 Astor Court   470 Astor Court
   III. Halprin, Phillip   Halperin, Phillip
   IV. Frank D. Poliseo   Frank D. Poliseo

3.   I.   Tandem Associates   Tandom Associates   3.____
   II. 144-17 Northern Blvd. 144-17 Northern Blvd.
   III. Alberta Forchi   Albert Forchi
   IV. Kings Park, NY 10751   Kings Point, NY 10751

4.   I.   Bertha C. McCormack   Bertha C. McCormack 4.____
   II. Clayton, MO   Clayton, MO
   III. 976-4242   976-4242
   IV. New City, NY 10951   New City, NY 10951

5.   I.   George C. Morill   George C. Morrill   5.____
   II. Columbia, SC 29201   Columbia, SD 29201
   III. Louis Ingham   Louis Ingham
   IV. 3406 Forest Ave.   3406 Forest Ave.

6.   I.   506 S. Elliott Pl.   506 S. Elliott Pl.   6.____
   II. Herbert Hall   Hurbert Hall
   III. 4712 Rockaway Pkway   4712 Rockaway Pkway
   IV. 169 E. 7 St.   169 E. 7 St.

7. I.   345 Park Ave.   345 Park Pl.   7._____
    II. Colman Oven Corp.   Coleman Oven Corp.
    III. Robert Conte   Robert Conti
    IV. 6179846   6179846

8. I.   Grigori Schierber   Grigori Schierber   8._____
    II. Des Moines, Iowa   Des Moines, Iowa
    III. Gouverneur Hospital   Gouverneur Hospital
    IV. 91-35 Cresskill Pl.   91-35 Cresskill Pl.

9. I.   Jeffery Janssen   Jeffrey Janssen   9._____
    II. 8041071   8041071
    III. 40 Rockefeller Plaza   40 Rockafeller Plaza
    IV. 407 6 St.   406 7 St.

10. I.   5971996   5871996   10._____
    II. 3113 Knickerbocker Ave.   31123 Knickerbocker Ave.
    III. 8434 Boston Post Rd.   8424 Boston Post Rd.
    IV. Penn Station   Penn Station

Questions 11-14.

DIRECTIONS: Questions 11 through 14 are to be answered by looking at the four groups of names and addresses listed below (I, II, III, and IV), and then finding out the number of groups that have their corresponding numbered lies exactly the same.

	GROUP I	GROUP II
Line 1.	Richmond General Hospital	Richman General Hospital
Line 2.	Geriatric Clinic	Geriatric Clinic
Line 3.	3975 Paerdegat St.	3975 Peardegat St.
Line 4.	Loudonville, New York 11538	Londonville, New York 11538

	GROUP III	GROUP IV
Line 1.	Richmond General Hospital	Richmend General Hospital
Line 2.	Geriatric Clinic	Geriatric Clinic
Line 3.	3795 Paerdegat St.	3975 Paerdegat St.
Line 4.	Loudonville, New York 11358	Loudonville, New York 11538

1. In how many groups is line one exactly the same?   11._____
    A. Two   B. Three   C. Four   D. None

12. In how many groups is line two exactly the same?   12._____
    A. Two   B. Three   C. Four   D. None

13. In how many groups is line three exactly the same?   13._____
    A. Two   B. Three   C. Four   D. None

14. In how many groups is line four exactly the same?   14._____
    A. Two   B. Three   C. Four   D. None

Questions 15-18.

DIRECTIONS: Each of Questions 15 through 18 has two lists of names and addresses. Each list contains three sets of names and addresses. Check each of the three sets in the list on the right to see if they are the same as the corresponding set in the list on the left. Mark your answers:
   A. if none of the sets in the right list are the same as those in the left list
   B. if only one of the sets in the right list is the same as those in the left list
   C. if only two of the sets in the right list are the same as those in the left list
   D. if all three sets in the right list are the same as those in the left list

15. Mary T. Berlinger   Mary T. Berlinger   15._____
    2351 Hampton St.   2351 Hampton St.
    Monsey, N.Y. 20117   Monsey, N.Y. 20117

    Eduardo Benes   Eduardo Benes
    483 Kingston Avenue   473 Kingston Avenue
    Central Islip, N.Y. 11734 Central Islip, N.Y. 11734

    Alan Carrington Fuchs   Alan Carrington Fuchs
    17 Gnarled Hollow Road   17 Gnarled Hollow Road
    Los Angeles, CA 91635   Los Angeles, CA 91685

16. David John Jacobson   David John Jacobson   16._____
    178 34 St. Apt. 4C   178 53 St. Apt. 4C
    New York, N.Y. 00927   New York, N.Y. 00927

    Ann-Marie Calonella   Ann-Marie Calonella
    7243 South Ridge Blvd.   7243 South Ridge Blvd.
    Bakersfield, CA 96714   Bakersfield, CA 96714

    Pauline M. Thompson   Pauline M. Thomson
    872 Linden Ave.   872 Linden Ave.
    Houston, Texas 70321   Houston, Texas 70321

17. Chester LeRoy Masterton   Chester LeRoy Masterson   17._____
    152 Lacy Rd.   152 Lacy Rd.
    Kankakee, Ill. 54532   Kankakee, Ill. 54532

    William Maloney   William Maloney
    S. LaCrosse Pla.   S. LaCross Pla.
    Wausau, Wisconsin 52136   Wausau, Wisconsin 52146

    Cynthia V. Barnes   Cynthia V. Barnes
    16 Pines Rd.   16 Pines Rd.
    Greenpoint, Miss. 20376   Greenpoint,, Miss. 20376

18. Marcel Jean Frontenac   Marcel Jean Frontenac   18.____
    8 Burton On The Water   6 Burton On The Water
    Calender, Me. 01471   Calender, Me. 01471

    J. Scott Marsden   J. Scott Marsden
    174 S. Tipton St.   174 Tipton St.
    Cleveland, Ohio   Cleveland, Ohio

    Lawrence T. Haney   Lawrence T. Haney
    171 McDonough St.   171 McDonough St.
    Decatur, Ga. 31304   Decatur, Ga. 31304

Questions 19-26.

DIRECTIONS: Each of Questions 19 through 26 has two lists of numbers. Each list contains three sets of numbers. Check each of the three sets in the list on the right to see if they are the same as the corresponding set in the list on the left. Mark your answers:
   A. if none of the sets in the right list are the same as those in the left list
   B. if only one of the sets in the right list is the same as those in the left list
   C. if only two of the sets in the right list are the same as those in the left list
   D. if all three sets in the right list are the same as those in the left lists

19. 7354183476   7354983476   19.____
    4474747744   4474747774
    5791430231   57914302311

20. 7143592185   7143892185   20.____
    8344517699   8344518699
    9178531263   9178531263

21. 2572114731   257214731   21.____
    8806835476   8806835476
    8255831246   8255831246

22. 331476853821   331476858621   22.____
    6976658532996   6976655832996
    3766042113715   3766042113745

23. 8806663315   88066633115   23.____
    74477138449   74477138449
    211756663666   211756663666

24. 990006966996   99000696996   24.____
     53022219743   53022219843
     4171171117717   4171171177717

25. 24400222433004   24400222433004   25.____
     5300030055000355   5300030055500355
     20000075532002022   20000075532002022

26. 6111666406600011 16 61116664066001116   26.____
     7111300117001100733 7111300117001100733
     26666446664476518   26666446664476518

Questions 27-30.

DIRECTIONS: Questions 27 through 30 are to be answered by picking the answer which is in the correct numerical order, from the lowest number to the highest number, in each question.

27. A. 44533, 44518, 44516, 44547   27.____
    B. 44516, 44518, 44533, 44547
    C. 44547, 44533, 44518, 44516
    D. 44518, 44516, 44547, 44533

28. A. 95587, 95593, 95601, 95620   28.____
    B. 95601, 95620, 95587, 95593
    C. 95593, 95587, 95601. 95620
    D. 95620, 95601, 95593, 95587

29. A. 232212, 232208, 232232, 232223   29.____
    B. 232208, 232223, 232212, 232232
    C. 232208, 232212, 232223, 232232
    D. 232223, 232232, 232208, 232208

30. A. 113419, 113521, 113462, 113462   30.____
    B. 113588, 113462, 113521, 113419
    C. 113521, 113588, 113419, 113462
    D. 113419, 113462, 113521, 113588

KEY (CORRECT ANSWERS)

1.	C	11.	A	21.	C
2.	B	12.	C	22.	A
3.	D	13.	A	23.	D
4.	A	14.	A	24.	A
5.	C	15.	C	25.	C
6.	B	16.	B	26.	C
7.	D	17.	B	27.	B
8.	A	18.	B	28.	A
9.	D	19.	B	29.	C
10.	C	20.	B	30.	D

BASIC FUNDAMENTALS OF FILING SCIENCE

TABLE OF CONTENTS

		Page
I.	COMMENTARY	1
II.	BASICS OF FILING	1
	1. Types of Files	1
	a. Shannon File	1
	b. Spindle File	1
	c. Box File	1
	d. Flat File	1
	e. Bellows File	1
	f. Vertical File	1
	g. Clip File	1
	h. Visible File	2
	i. Rotary File	2
	2. Aids in Filing	2
	3. Variations of Filing Systems	2
	4. Centralized Filing	2
	5. Methods of Filing	3
	a. Alphabetic Filing	3
	b. Subject Filing	3
	c. Geographical Filing	3
	d. Chronological Filing	3
	e. Numerical Filing	3
	6. Indexing	3
	7. Alphabetizing	4
III.	RULES FOR INDEXING AND ALPHABETIZING	4
IV.	OFFICIAL EXAMINATION DIRECTIONS AND RULES	8
	1. Official Directions	8
	2. Official Rules For Alphabetical Filing	9
	a. Names of Individuals	9
	b. Names of Business Organizations	9
	3. Sample Question	9

BASIC FUNDAMENTALS OF FILING SCIENCE

I. COMMENTARY

    Filing is the systematic arrangement and storage of papers, cards, forms, catalogues, etc. so that they may be found easily and quickly. The importance of an efficient filing system cannot be emphasized too strongly. The filed materials form records which may be needed quickly to settle questions that may cause embarrassing situations if such evidence is not available. In addition to keeping papers in order so that they are readily available, the filing system must also be designed to keep papers in good condition. A filing system must be planned so that papers may be filed easily, withdrawn easily, and as quickly returned to their proper place. The cost of a filing system is also an important factor
    The need for a filing system arose when the businessman began to carry on negotiations on a large scale. He could no longer be intimate with the details of his business. What was needed in the early era was a spindle or pigeon-hole desk. Filing in pigeon-hole desks is now almost completely extinct. It was an unsatisfactory practice since pigeon holes were not labeled, and the desk was an untidy mess.

II. BASIS OF FILING

The science of filing is an exact one and entails a thorough understanding of basic facts, materials, and methods. An overview of this important information now follows.

    1. Types of Files

        a. Shannon File: This consists of a board, at one end of which are fastened two arches which may be opened laterally.

        b. Spindle File: This consists of a metal or wood base to which is attached a long, pointed spike. Papers are pushed down on the spike as received. This file is useful for temporary retention of papers.

        c. Box File: This is a heavy cardboard or metal box, opening from the side like a book.

        d. Flat File: This consists of a series of shallow drawers or trays, arranged like drawers in a cabinet.

        e. Bellows File: This is a heavy cardboard container with alphabetized or compartment sections, the ends of which are enclosed in such a manner that they resemble an accordion.

        f. Vertical File: This consists of one or more drawers in which the papers are stood on edge, usually in folders, and are indexed by guides. A series of two or more drawers in one unit is the usual file cabinet.

        g. Clip File: This file has a large clip attached to a board and is very similar to the Shannon File.

h. Visible File: Cards are filed flat in an overlapping arrangement which leaves a part of each card visible at all times.

i. Rotary File: The rotary file has a number of visible card files attached to a post around which they can be revolved. The wheel file has visible cards which rotate around a horizontal axis.

j. Tickler File: This consists of cards or folders marked with the days of the month, in which materials are filed and turned up on the appropriate day of the month.

2. Aids in Filing

   a. Guides: Guides are heavy cardboard, pasteboard, or Bristol-board sheets the same size as folders. At the top is a tab on which is marked or printed the distinguishing letter, words, or numbers indicating the material filed in a section of the drawer.

   b. Sorting Trays: Sorting trays are equipped with alphabetical guides to facilitate the sorting of papers preparatory to placing them in a file.

   c. Coding: Once the classification or indexing caption has been determined, it must be indicated on the letter for filing purposes.

   d. Cross-Reference: Some letters or papers might easily be called for under two or more captions. For this purpose, a cross-reference card or sheet is placed in the folder or in the index.

3. Variations of Filing Systems

   a. Variadex Alphabetic Index: Provides for more effective expansion of the alphabetic system.

   b. Triple-Check Numeric Filing: Entails a multiple cross-reference, as the name implies.

   c. Variadex Filing: Makes use of color as an aid in filing.

   d. Dewey Decimal System: The system is a numeric one used in libraries or for filing library materials in an office. This special type of filing system is used where material is grouped in finely divided categories, such as in libraries. With this method, all material to be filed is divided into ten major groups, from 000 to 900, and then subdivided into tens, units, and decimals.

4. Centralized Filing

Centralized filing means keeping the files in one specific or central location. Decentralized filing means putting away papers in files of individual departments. The first step in the organization of a central filing department is to make a careful canvass of all desks in the offices. In this manner we can determine just what material needs to be filed, and what information each desk occupant requires from the central file. Only papers which may be used at some time by persons in the various offices should be placed in the central file. A paper that is to be used at some time by persons in the various offices should be placed in the central file. A paper that is to be used by one department only should never be filed in the central file.

5. Methods of Filing

   While there are various methods used for filing, actually there are only five basic systems: alphabetical, subject, numerical, geographic, and chronological. All other systems are derived from one of these or from a combination of two or more of them. Since the purpose of a filing system is to store business records systemically so that any particular record can be found almost instantly when required, filing requires, in addition to the proper kinds of equipment and supplies, an effective method of indexing.
   There are five basic systems of filing:

   a. Alphabetic Filing: Most filing is alphabetical. Other methods, as described below, require extensive alphabetization. In alphabetical filing, lettered dividers or guides are arranged in alphabetic sequence. Material to be filed is placed behind the proper guide. All materials under each letter are also arranged alphabetically. Folders are used unless the file is a card index.

   b. Subject Filing: This method is used when a single, complete file on a certain subject is desired. A subject file is often maintained to assemble all correspondence on a certain subject. Such files are valuable in connection with insurance claims, contract negotiations, personnel, and other investigations, special programs, and similar subjects.

   c. Geographical File: Materials are filed according to location: states, cities, counties, or other subdivisions. Statistics and tax information are often filed in this manner.

   d. Chronological File: Records are filed according to date. This method is used especially in "tickler" files that have guides numbered 1 to 31 for each day of the month. Each number indicates the day of the month when the filed item requires attention.

   e. Numerical File: This method requires an alphabetic card index giving name and number. The card index is used to locate records numbered consecutively in the files according to date received or sequence in which issued, such as licenses, permits, etc.

6. Indexing

   Determining the name or title under which an item is to be filed is known as indexing. For example, how would a letter from Robert E. Smith be filed? The name would be rearranged Smith, Robert E., so that the letter would be filed under the last name.

7. Alphabetizing

The arranging of names for filing is known as alphabetizing. For example, suppose you have four letters indexed under the names Johnson, Becker, Roe, and Stern. How should these letters be arranged in the files so that they may be found easily? You would arrange the four names alphabetically, thus Becker, Johnson, Roe, and Stern.

III. RULES FOR INDEXING AND ALPHABETIZING

1. The names of persons are to be transposed. Write the surname first, then the given name, and, finally, the middle name or initial. Then arrange the various names according to the alphabetic order of letters throughout the entire name. If there is a title, consider that after the middle name or initial.

NAMES	INDEXED AS
Arthur L. Bright	Bright, Arthur L.
Arthur S. Bright	Bright, Arthur S.
P.E. Cole	Cole, P.E.
Dr. John C. Fox	Fox, John C. (Dr.)

2. If a surname includes the same letters of another surname, with one or more additional letters added to the end, the shorter surname is placed first regardless of the given name or the initial of the given name.

NAMES	INDEXED AS
Robert E. Brown	Brown, Robert E.
Gerald A. Browne	Browne, Gerald A.
William O. Brownell	Brownell, William O.

3. Firm names are alphabetized under the surnames. Words like the, an, a, of, and for, are not considered.

NAMES	INDEXED AS
Bank of America	Bank of America
Bank Discount Dept.	Bank Discount Dept.
The Cranford Press	Cranford Press, The
Nelson Dwyer & Co.	Dwyer, Nelson, & Co.
Sears, Roebuck & Co.	Sears Roebuck & Co.
Montgomery Ward & Co.	Ward, Montgomery, & Co.

4. The order of filing is determined first of all by the first letter of the names to be filed. If the first letters are the same, the order is determined by the second letters, and so on. In the following pairs of names, the order is determined by the letters underlined:

   | <u>A</u>usten | H<u>a</u>yes | Ha<u>n</u>son | Har<u>ve</u>y | Hea<u>th</u> | Gree<u>n</u> | Schwar<u>tz</u> |
   | <u>B</u>aker | H<u>e</u>ath | Ha<u>r</u>per | Har<u>w</u>ood | Hea<u>to</u>n | Gree<u>ne</u> | Schwar<u>z</u> |

5. When surnames are alike, those with initials only precede those with given names, unless the first initial comes alphabetically after the first letter of the name.

Gleason, S.	*but*, Abbott, Mary
Gleason, S.W.	Abbott, W.B.
Gleason, Sidney	

6. Hyphenated names are treated as if spelled without the hyphen.
Lloyd, Paul N.	Lloyd, Robert
Lloyd-Jones, James	Lloyd-Thomas, A.S.

7. Company names composed of single letters which are not used as abbreviations precede the other names beginning with the same letter.
B & S Garage	E Z Duplicator Co.
B X Cable Co.	Eagle Typewriter Co.
Babbitt, R.N.	Edison Company

8. The ampersand (&) and the apostrophe (') in firm names are disregarded in alphabetizing.
Nelson & Niller	M & C Amusement Corp.
Nelson, Walter J.	M C Art Assn.
Nelson's Bakery	

9. Names beginning with Mac, Mc, or M' are usually placed in regular order as spelled. Some filing systems file separately names beginning with Mc.
MacDonald, R.J.	Mazza, Anthony
MacDonald, S.B.	McAdam, Wm.
Mace, Wm.	McAndrews, Jerry

10. Names beginning with St. are listed as if the name Saint were spelled in full. Numbered street names and all abbreviated names are treated as if spelled out in full.
Saginaw	Fifth Avenue Hotel	Hart Mfg. Co.
St. Louis	42nd Street Dress Shop	Hart, Martin
St. Peter's Rectory	Hart, Chas.	Hart, Thos.
Sandford	Hart, Charlotte	Hart, Thomas A.
Smith, Wm.	Hart, Jas.	Hart, Thos. R.
Smith, Willis	Hart, Janice	

11. Federal, state, or city departments of government should be placed alphabetically under the governmental branch controlling them.

    Illinois, State of – Departments and Commissions
        Banking Dept.
        Employment Bureau
    United States Government Departments
        Commerce
        Defense
        State
        Treasury

12. Alphabetic Order: Each word in a name is an indexing unit. Arrange the names in alphabetic order by comparing similar units in each name. Consider the second units only when the first units are identical. Consider the third units only when both the first and second units are identical.

13. Single Surnames or Initials: A surname, when used alone, precedes the same surname with a first name or initial. A surname with a first initial only precedes a surname with a complete first name. This rule is sometimes stated, "nothing comes before something."

14. Surname Prefixes: A surname prefix is not a separate indexing unit, but it is considered part of the surname. These prefixes include: d', D', Da, de, De, Del, Des, Di, Du, Fitz., La, Le, Mc, Mac, 'c, O', St., Van, Van der, Von, Von der, and others. The prefixes M', Mac, and Mc are indexed and filed exactly as they are spelled.

15. Names of Firms: Names of firms and institutions are indexed and filed exactly as they are written when they do not contain the complete name of an individual.

16. Names of Firms Containing Complete Individual Names: When the firm or institution name includes the complete name of an individual, the units are transposed for indexing in the same way as the name of an individual.

17. Article "The": When the article "the" occurs at the beginning of a name, it is placed at the end in parentheses but it is not moved. In both cases, it is not an indexing unit and is disregarded in filing.

18. Hyphenated Names: Hyphenated firm names are considered as separate indexing units. Hyphenated surnames of individuals are considered as one indexing unit; this applies also to hyphenated names of individuals whose complete names are part of a firm name.

19. Abbreviations: Abbreviations are considered as though the name were written in full; however, single letters other than abbreviations are considered as separate indexing units.

20. Conjunctions, Prepositions, and Firm Endings: Conjunctions and prepositions, such as and, for, in, of, are disregarded in indexing and filing but are not omitted or their order changed when writing names on cards and folders. Firm endings, such as Ltd., Inc., So., Son, Bros., Mfg., and Corp., are treated as a unit in indexing and filing and are considered as though spelled in full, such as Brothers and Incorporated.

21. One of Two Words: Names that may be spelled either as one or two words are indexed and filed as one word.

22. Compound Geographic Names: Compound geographic names are considered as separate indexing and filing units, except when the first part of the name is not an English word, such as the Los in Los Angeles.

23. Titles or degrees of individuals, whether preceding or following the name, are not considered in indexing or filing. They are placed in parentheses after the given name or initial. Terms that designate seniority, such as Jr., Sr., 2d, are also placed in parentheses and are considered for indexing and filing only when the names to be indexed are otherwise identical.

Exception A: When the name of an individual consists of a title and one name only, such as Queen Elizabeth, it is not transposed and the title is considered for indexing and filing.

Exception B: When a title or foreign article is the initial word of a firm or association name, it is considered for indexing and filing.

24. Possessives: When a word ends in apostrophe s, the s is not considered in indexing and filing. However, when a word ends in s apostrophe, because the s is part of the original word, it is considered. This rule is sometimes stated, "Consider everything up to the apostrophe."

25. United States and Foreign Government Names: Names pertaining to the federal government are indexed and filed under United States Government and then subdivided by title of the department, bureau, division, commission, or board. Names pertaining to foreign governments are indexed and filed under names of countries and then subdivided by title of the department, bureau, division, commission, or board. Phrases, such as department of, bureau of, division of, commission of, board of, when used in titles of governmental bodies, are placed in parentheses after the word they modify, but are disregarded in indexing and filing. Such phrases, however, are considered in indexing and filing governmental names.

26. Other Political Subdivisions: Names pertaining to other political subdivisions, such as states, counties, cities, or towns, are indexed and filed under the name of the political subdivision and then subdivided by the title of the department, bureau, division, commission, or board.

27. When the same name appears with different addresses, the names are indexed as usual and arranged alphabetically according to city or town. The State is considered only when there is duplication of both individual or company name and city name. If the same name is located at different addresses within the same city, then the names are arranged alphabetically by streets. If the same name is located at more than one address on the same street then the names are arranged from the lower to the higher street number.

28. Numbers: Any number in a name is considered as though it were written in words, and it is indexed and filed as one unit.

29. Bank Names: Because the names of many banking institutions are alike in several respects, as First National Bank, Second National Bank, etc., banks are indexed and filed first by city location, then by bank name, with the state location written in parentheses and considered only if necessary.

30. Married Women: The legal name of a married woman is the one used for filing purposes. Legally, a man's surname is the only part of a man's name a woman assumes when she marries. Her legal name, therefore, could be either:
    a. Her own first and middle names together with her husband's surname, or
    b. Her own first name and maiden surname, together with her husband's surname.

Mrs. is placed in parentheses at the end of the name. Her husband's first and middle names are given in parentheses below her legal name.

31. An alphabetically arranged list of names illustrating many difficult points of alphabetizing follows:

COLUMN I	COLUMN II
Abbot, W.B.	54th St. Tailor Shop
Abbot, Alice	Forstall, W.J.
Allen Alexander B.	44th St. Garage
Allen, Alexander B., Inc.	M A Delivery Co.
Andersen, Hans	M & C Amusement Corp.
Andersen, Hans E.	M C Art Assn.
Andersen, Hans E., Jr.	MacAdam, Wm.
Anderson, Andrew Andrews,	Macaulay, James
George Brown Motor Co., Boston	MacAulay, Wilson
Brown Motor Co., Chicago	MacDonald, R.J.
Brown Motor Co., Philadelphia	Macdonald, S. B.
Brown Motor Co., San Francisco	Mace, Wm.
Dean, Anna	Mazza, Anthony
Dean, Anna F.	McAdam, Wm.
Dean, Anna Frances	McAndrews, Jerry
Dean & Co.	Meade & Clark Co.
Deane-Arnold Apartments	Meade, S.T.
Deane's Pharmacy	Meade, Soloman
Deans, Felix A.	Sackett Publishing Co.
Dean's Studio	Sacks, Robert
Deans, Wm.	St. Andrew Hotel
Deans & Williams	St. John, Homer W.
East Randolph	Saks, Isaac B.
East St. Louis	Stephens, Ira
Easton, Pa.	Stevens, Delevan
Eastport, Me.	Stevens, Delila

IV. OFFICIAL EXAMINATION DIRECTIONS AND RULES

To preclude the possibility of conflicting or varying methods of filing, explicit directions and express rules are given to the candidate before he answers the filing questions on an examination.
The most recent official directions and rules for the filing questions are given immediately hereafter.

OFFICIAL DIRECTIONS

Each of questions…to…consists of four (five) names. For each question, select the one of the four(five) names that should be first (second)(third)(last) if the four (five(names were arranged in alphabetical order in accordance with the rules for alphabetical filing given below. Read these rules carefully. Then, for each question, indicate in the correspondingly numbered row on the answer sheet the letter preceding the name that should be first(second)(third)(last) in alphabetical order.

OFFICIAL RULES FOR ALPHABETICAL FILING

Names of Individuals

1. The names of individuals are filed in strict alphabetical order, first according to the last name, then according to first name or initial, and, finally, according to middle name or initial. For example: William Jones precedes George Kirk and Arthur S. Blake precedes Charles M. Blake.
2. When the last names are identical, the one with an initial instead of a first name precedes the one "with a first name beginning with the same initial." For example: J. Green precedes Joseph Green.
3. When identical last names also have identical first names, the one without a middle name or initial precedes the one with a middle name or initial. For example: Robert Jackson precedes both Robert C. Jackson and Robert Chester Jackson.
4. When last names are identical and the first names are also identical, the one with a middle initial precedes the one with a middle name beginning with the same initial. For example: Peter A. Brown precedes Peter Alvin Brown.
5. Prefixes such as De, El, La, and Van are considered parts of the names they precede. For example: Wilfred DeWald precedes Alexander Duval.
6. Last names beginning with "Mac" or "Mc" are filed as spelled.
7. Abbreviated names are treated as if they were spelled out. For example: Jos. is filed as Joseph and Robt. is filed as Robert.
8. Titles and designations such as Dr., Mrs., Prof. are disregarding in filing.

Names of Business Organizations

1. The names of business organizations are filed exactly as written, except that an organization bearing the name of an individual is filed alphabetically according to the name of the individual in accordance with the rules for filing names of individuals given above. For example: Thomas Allison Machine Company precedes Northern Baking Company.
2. When numerals occur in a name, they are treated as if they were spelled out. For example: 6 stands for six and 4th stands for fourth.
3. When the following words occur in names, they are disregarded: the, of

SAMPLE QUESTION

Choose the name that should be filed third.
A. Fred Town (2)   B. Jack Towne (3)   C. D. Town (1)   D. Jack Stone (4)
The numbers in parentheses indicate the proper alphabetical order in which these names should be filed. Since the name that should be filed <u>third</u> is Jack Towne, the answer is (B).

FILING

EXAMINATION SECTION
TEST 1

DIRECTIONS: Each question from 1 through 10 contains four names. For each question, choose the name that should be FIRST if the four names were arranged in alphabetical order in accordance with the Rules for Alphabetical Filing given before. Read these rules carefully. Then, for each question, print in the space at the right the letter before the name that should be FIRST in alphabetical order.

SAMPLE QUESTION
A. Jane Earl   (2)
B. James A. Earle   (4)
C. James Earl   (1)
D. J. Earle   (3)

The numbers in parentheses show the proper alphabetical order in which these names should be filed. Since the name that should be filed FIRST is James Earl, the answer to the sample question is C.

1. A. Majorca Leather Goods
   B. Robert Maiorca and Sons
   C. Maintenance Management Corp.
   D. Majestic Carpet Mills

   1.____

2. A. Municipal Telephone Service
   B. Municipal Reference Library
   C. Municipal Credit Union
   D. Municipal Broadcasting System

   2.____

3. A. Robert B. Pierce   B. R. Bruce Pierce
   C. Ronald Pierce   D. Robert Bruce Pierce

   3.____

4. A. Four Seasons Sports Club
   B. 14 Street Shopping Center
   C. Forty Thieves Restaurant
   D. 42nd St. Theaters

   4.____

5. A. Franco Franceschini   B. Amos Franchini
   C. Sandra Franceschia   D. Lilie Franchinesca

   5.____

6. A. Chas. A. Levine   B. Kurt Levene
   C. Charles Levine   D. Kurt E. Levene

   6.____

7. A. Prof. Geo. Kinkaid   B. Mr. Alan Kinkaid
   C. Dr. Albert A. Kinkade   D. Kincade Liquors Inc.

   7.____

8. A. Department of Public Events
    B. Office of the Public Administrator
    C. Queensborough Public Library
    D. Department of Public Health

9. A. Martin Luther King, Jr. Towers
    B. Metro North Plaza
    C. Manhattanville Houses
    D. Marble Hill Houses

10. A. Dr. Arthur Davids
    B. The David Check Cashing Service
    C. A. C. Davidsen
    D. Milton Davidoff

KEY (CORRECT ANSWERS)

1. C
2. D
3. B
4. D
5. C

6. B
7. D
8. B
9. A
10. B

TEST 2

DIRECTIONS: Each of questions 1 to 10 consists of four names. For each question, select the one of the four names that should be THIRD if the four names were arranged in alphabetical order in accordance with the Rules of Alphabetical Filing given before. Read these rules carefully. Then, for each question, print in the space at the right the letter preceding the name that should be THIRD in alphabetical order.

SAMPLE QUESTION

    A. Fred Town   (2)
    B. Jack Towne   (3)
    C. D. Town   (1)
    D. Jack S. Towne   (4)

The numbers in parentheses indicate the proper alphabetical order in which these names should be filed. Since the name that should be filed THIRD is Jack Towne, the answer is B.

1. A. Herbert Restman   B. H. Restman
   C. Harry Restmore   D. H. Restmore

2. A. Martha Eastwood   B. Martha E. Eastwood
   C. Martha Edna Eastwood   D. M. Eastwood

3. A. Timothy Macalan   B. Fred McAlden
   C. Thomas MacAllister   D. Mrs. Frank McAllen

4. A. Elm Trading Co.
   B. El Dorado Trucking Corp.
   C. James Eldred Jewelry Store
   D. Eldridge Printing, Inc.

5. A. Edward La Gabriel   B. Marie Doris Gabriel
   C. Marjorie N. Gabriel   D. Mrs. Marian Gabriel

6. A. Peter La Vance   B. George Van Meer
   C. Wallace De Vance   D. Leonard Vance

7. A. Fifth Avenue Book Shop
   B. Mr. Wm. A. Fifner
   C. 52nd Street Association
   D. Robert B. Fiffner

8. A. Dr. Chas. D. Peterson   B. Miss Irene F. Petersen
   C. Lawrence E. Peterson   D. Prof. N. A. Petersen

9. A. 71st Street Theater   B. The Seven Seas Corp.
   C. 7th Ave. Service Co.   D. Walter R. Sevan and Co.

10. A. Aerol Auto Body, Inc.
    B. AAB Automotive Service Corp.
    C. Acer Automotive
    D. Alerte Automotive Corp.

10.____

KEY (CORRECT ANSWERS)

1. D
2. B
3. B
4. D
5. C

6. D
7. A
8. A
9. C
10. A

TEST 3

DIRECTIONS: Same as for Test 2.

1. A. William Carver B. Howard Cambell
   C. Arthur Chambers D. Charles Banner
   1._____

2. A. Paul Moore B. William Moore
   C. Paul A. Moore D. William Allen Moore
   2._____

3. A. George Peters B. Eric Petersen
   C. G. Peters D. E. Petersen
   3._____

4. A. Edward Hallam B. Jos. Frank Hamilton
   C. Edward A. Hallam D. Joseph F. Hamilton
   4._____

5. A. Theodore Madison B. Timothy McGill
   C. Thomas MacLane D. Thomas A. Madison
   5._____

6. A. William O'Hara B. Arthur Gordon
   C. James DeGraff D. Anne von Glatin
   6._____

7. A. Charles Green B. Chas. T. Greene
   C. Charles Thomas Greene D. Wm. A. Greene
   7._____

8. A. John Foss Insurance Co. B. New World Stove Co.
   C. 14th Street Dress Shop D. Arthur Stein Paper Co.
   8._____

9. A. Gold Trucking Co. B. B. 8th Ave. Garage
   C. The First National Bank D. The Century Novelty Co.
   9._____

10. A. F. L. Doskow B. Natalie S. Doskow
    C. Samuel B. Doskow D. Arthur G. Doskor
    10._____

KEY (CORRECT ANSWERS)

1. A
2. B
3. D
4. D
5. D

6. A
7. C
8. B
9. C
10. B

TEST 4

DIRECTIONS: Each question from 1 through 10 consists of four names. For each question, choose the one of the four names that should be *LAST* if the four names were arranged in alphabetical order in accordance with the Rules for Alphabetical Filing given before. Read these rules carefully. Then, for each question, print in the space at the right the letter before the name that should be *LAST* in alphabetical order.

SAMPLE QUESTION

  A. Jane Earl (2)
  B. James A. Earle (4)
  C. James Earl (1)
  D. J. Earle (3)

The numbers in parentheses show the proper alphabetical order in which these names should be filed. Since the name that should be filed *LAST* is James A. Earle, the answer to the sample question is B.

1. A. Corral, Dr. Robert B. Carrale, Prof. Robert
  C. Corren, R. D. Corret, Ron

2. A. Rivera, Ilena B. Riviera, Ilene
  C. Rivere, I. D. Riviera Ice-Cream Co.

3. A. VonHogel, George B. Volper, Gary
  C. Vonner, G. D. Van Pefel, Gregory

4. A. David Kallish Stationery Co.
  B. Emerson Microfilm Company
  C. David Kalder Industrial Engineers Associated
  D. 5th Avenue Office Furniture Co.

5. A. A. Bennet, C. B. Benett, Chuck
  C. Bennet, Chas. D. Bennett, Charles

6. A. The Board of Higher Education
  B. National Education Commission
  C. Eakin, Hugh
  D. Nathan, Ellen

7. A. McCloud, I. B. MacGowen, Ian
  C. McGowen, Arthur D. Macale, Sean

8. A. Devine, Sarah B. Devine, S.
  C. Devine, Sara H. D. Devin, Sarah

9. A. Milstein, Louis B. Milrad, Abraham P.
  C. Milstein, Herman D. Milstien, Harold G.

10. A. Herfield, Lester L. B. Herbstman, Nathan
  C. Henricksen, Ole A. D. Herfeld, Burton G.

KEY (CORRECT ANSWERS)

1. D
2. B
3. C
4. A
5. D

6. B
7. C
8. A
9. D
10. A

———

TEST 5

DIRECTIONS: Same as for Test 4.

1. A. Francis Lattimore   B. H. Latham
   C. G. Lattimore   D. Hugh Latham   1.____

2. A. Thomas B. Morgan   B. B. Thomas Morgan
   C. T. Morgan   D. Thomas Bertram Morgan   2.____

3. A. Lawrence A. Villon   B. Chas. Valente
   C. Charles M. Valent   D. Lawrence De Villon   3.____

4. A. Alfred Devance   B. A. R. D'Amico
   C. Arnold De Vincent   D. A. De Pino   4.____

5. A. Dr. Milton A. Bergmann B. Miss Evelyn M. Bergmenn
   C. Prof. E. N. Bergmenn   D. Mrs. L. B. Bergmann   5.____

6. A. George MacDougald   B. Thomas McHern
   C. William Macholt   D. Frank McHenry   6.____

7. A. Third National Bank   B. Robt. Tempkin Corp.
   C. 32nd Street Carpet Co. D. Wm. Templeton, Inc.   7.____

8. A. Mary Lobell Art Shop   B. John La Marca, Inc
   C. Lawyers' Guild   D. Frank Le Goff Studios   8.____

9. A. 9th Avenue Garage   B. Jos. Nuren Food Co.
   C. The New Book Store   D. Novelty Card Corp.   9.____

10. A. Murphy's Moving & Storage, Inc.   10.____
    B. Mid-Island Van Lines Corporation
    C. Mollone Bros. Moving & Storage, Inc.
    D. McShane Moving & Storage, Inc.

KEY (CORRECT ANSWERS)

1. C
2. D
3. A
4. C
5. B
6. B
7. C
8. A
9. B
10. A

TEST 6

DIRECTIONS: Each question contains four names numbered from 1 through 4 but not necessarily numbered in correct filing order. Answer each question by choosing the letter corresponding to the CORRECT filing order of the four names in accordance with the Rules for Alphabetic Filing given before. *PRINT THE LETTER OF THE CORRECT ANSWER IN THE SPACE AT THE RIGHT.*

SAMPLE QUESTION

1. Robert J. Smith
2. R. Jeffrey Smith
3. Dr. A. Smythe
4. Allen R. Smithers

A. 1, 2, 3, 4   B. 3, 1, 2, 4   C. 2, 1, 4, 3   D. 3, 2, 1, 4

Since the correct filing order, in accordance with the above rules, is 2, 1, 4, 3, the correct answer is C.

1.
   1. J. Chester VanClief
   2. John C. VanClief
   3. J. VanCleve
   4. Mary L. Vance

   A. 4, 3, 1, 2   B. 4, 3, 2, 1   C. 3, 1, 2, 4   D. 3, 4, 1, 2

2.
   1. Community Development Agency
   2. Department of Social Services
   3. Board of Estimate
   4. Bureau of Gas and Electricity

   A. 3, 4, 1, 2   B. 1, 2, 4, 3   C. 2, 1, 3, 4   D. 1, 3, 4, 2

3.
   1. Dr. Chas. K. Dahlman
   2. F. & A. Delivery Service
   3. Department of Water Supply
   4. Demano Men's Custom Tailors

   A. 1, 2, 3, 4   B. 1, 4, 2, 3   C. 4, 1, 2, 3   D. 4, 1, 3, 2

4.
   1. 48th Street Theater
   2. Fourteenth Street Day Care Center
   3. Professor A. Cartwright
   4. Albert F. McCarthy

   A. 4, 2, 1, 3   B. 4, 3, 1, 2   C. 3, 2, 1, 4   D. 3, 1, 2, 4

5.
   1. Frances D'Arcy
   2. Mario L. DelAmato
   3. William H. Diamond
   4. Robert J. DuBarry

   A. 1, 2, 4, 3   B. 2, 1, 3, 4   C. 1, 2, 3, 4   D. 2, 1, 3, 4

6.
   1. Evelyn H. D'Amelio
   2. Jane R. Bailey
   3. Robert Bailey
   4. Frank Baily

   A. 1, 2, 3, 4   B. 1, 3, 2, 4   C. 2, 3, 4, 1   D. 3, 2, 4, 1

7.
   1. Department of Markets
   2. Bureau of Handicapped Children
   3. Housing Authority Administration Building
   4. Board of Pharmacy

2 (#6)

      A. 2,1,3,4   B. 1,2,4,3   C. 1,2,3,4   D. 3,2,1,4

8. 1. William A. Shea Stadium
    2. Rapid Speed Taxi Co.
    3. Harry Stampler's Rotisserie
    4. Wilhelm Albert Shea

    A. 2, 3, 4, 1   B. 4, 1, 3, 2   C. 2, 4, 1, 3   D. 3, 4, 1, 2

9. 1. Robert S. Aaron, M. D.   2. Mrs. Norma S. Aaron
    3. Irving I. Aronson   4. Darius P. Aanonsen

    A. 1, 2, 3, 4   B. 2, 4, 1, 3   C. 4, 2, 3, 1   D. 4, 2, 1, 3

10. 1. The Gamut   2. Gilliar Drug Co., Inc.
    3. Georgette Cosmetology   4. Great Nock Pharmacy

    A. 1, 3, 2, 4   B. 3, 1, 4, 2   C. 1, 2, 3, 4   D. 1, 3, 4, 2

KEY (CORRECT ANSWERS)

1. A
2. D
3. B
4. D
5. C

6. D
7. D
8. C
9. D
10. A

TEST 7

DIRECTIONS: Each question consists of four names grouped vertically under four different filing arrangements lettered A, B, C, and D. In each question only one of the four arrangements lists the names in the correct filing order according to the Rules for Alphabetical Filing given before. Read these rules carefully. Then, for each question, select the correct filing arrangement, lettered A, B, C, or D and print in the space at the right the letter of that correct filing arrangement.

SAMPLE QUESTION

Arrangement A	Arrangement B	Arrangement C	Arrangement D
Arnold Robinson	Arthur Roberts	Arnold Robinson	Arthur Roberts
Arthur Roberts	J. B. Robin	Arthur Roberts	James Robin
J. B. Robin	James Robin	James Robin	J. B. Robin
James Robin	Arnold Robinson	J. B. Robin	Arnold Robinson

Since, in this sample, ARRANGEMENT B is the only one in which the four names are correctly arranged alphabetically, the answer is B.

1. *Arrangement A*
   Alice Thompson
   Arnold G. Thomas
   B. Thomas
   Eugene Thompkins
   Arrangement C
   B. Thomas Arnold
   G. Thomas
   Eugene Thompkins
   Alice Thompson

   Arrangement B
   Eugene Thompkins
   Alice Thompson
   Arnold G. Thomas
   B. Thomas
   Arrangement D
   Arnold G. Thomas
   B. Thomas
   Eugene Thompkins
   Alice Thompson

   1.____

2. *Arrangement A*
   Albert Green
   A. B. Green
   Frank E. Green
   Wm. Greenfield
   Arrangement C
   Albert Green
   Wm. Greenfield
   A. B. Green
   Frank E. Green

   Arrangement B
   A. B. Green
   Albert Green
   Frank E. Green
   Wm. Greenfield
   Arrangement D
   A. B. Green
   Frank E. Green
   Albert Green
   Wm. Greenfield

   2.____

3. *Arrangement A*
   Steven M. Comte
   Robt. Count
   Robert B. Count
   Steven Le Comte
   Arrangement C
   Steven M. Comte
   Steven Le Comte
   Robt. Count
   Robert B. Count

   Arrangement B
   Steven Le Comte
   Steven M. Comte
   Robert B. Count
   Robt. Count
   Arrangement D
   Robt. Count
   Robert B. Count
   Steven Le Comte
   Steven M. Comte

   3.____

4. *Arrangement A*
   Prof. David Towner
   Miss Edna Tower
   Dr. Frank I. Tower
   Mrs. K. C. Towner
   Arrangement C
   Miss Edna Tower
   Dr. Frank I. Tower
   Prof. David Towner
   Mrs. K. C. Towner

   Arrangement B
   Dr. Frank I. Tower
   Miss Edna Tower
   Mrs. K. C. Towner
   Prof. David Towner
   Arrangement D
   Prof. David Towner
   Mrs. K. C. Towner
   Miss Edna Tower
   Dr. Frank I. Tower

   4.____

5. *Arrangement A*
   The Jane Miller Shop
   Joseph Millard Corp.
   John Muller & Co.
   Jean Mullins, Inc.
   Arrangement C
   The Jane Miller Shop
   Jean Mullins, Inc.
   John Muller & Co.
   Joseph Millard Corp.

   Arrangement B
   Joseph Millard Corp.
   The Jane Miller Shop
   John Muller & Co.
   Jean Mullins, Inc.
   Arrangement D
   Joseph Millard Corp.
   John Muller & Co.
   Jean Mullins, Inc.
   The Jane Miller Shop

   5.____

6. *Arrangement A*
   Anthony Delaney
   A. M. D'Elia
   A. De Landri
   Alfred De Monte
   Arrangement C
   A. De Landri
   A. M. D'Elia
   Alfred De Monte
   Anthony Delaney

   Arrangement B
   Anthony Delaney
   A. De Landri
   A. M. D'Elia
   Alfred De Monte
   Arrangement D
   A. De Landri
   Anthony Delaney
   A. M. D'Elia
   Alfred De Monte

   6.____

7. *Arrangement A*
   D. McAllen
   Lewis McBride
   Doris MacAllister
   Lewis T. Mac Bride
   Arrangement C
   Doris MacAllister
   Lewis T. MacBride
   D. McAllen
   Lewis McBride

   Arrangement B
   D. McAllen
   Doris MacAllister
   Lewis McBride
   Lewis T. MacBride
   Arrangement D
   Doris MacAllister
   D. McAllen
   Lewis T. MacBride
   Lewis McBride

   7.____

8. *Arrangement A*
   6th Ave. Swim Shop
   The Sky Ski School
   Sport Shoe Store
   23rd Street Salon
   Arrangement C
   6th Ave. Swim Shop
   Sport Shoe Store
   The Sky Ski School
   23rd Street Salon

   Arrangement B
   23rd Street Salon
   The Sky Ski School
   6th Ave. Swim Shop
   Sport Shoe Store
   Arrangement D
   The Sky Ski School
   6th Ave. Swim Shop
   Sport Shoe Store
   23rd Street Salon

   8._____

9. *Arrangement A*
   Charlotte Stair
   C. B. Stare
   Charles B. Stare
   Elaine La Stella
   Arrangement C
   Elaine La Stella
   Charlotte Stair
   C. B. Stare
   Charles B. Stare

   Arrangement B
   C. B. Stare
   Charles B. Stare
   Charlotte Stair
   Elaine La Stella
   Arrangement D
   Charles B. Stare
   C. B. Stare
   Charlotte Stair
   Elaine La Stella

   9._____

10. *Arrangement A*
    John O'Farrell Corp.
    Finest Glass Co.
    George Fraser Co.
    4th Guarantee Bank
    Arrangement C
    John O'Farrell Corp.
    Finest Glass Co.
    4th Guarantee Bank
    George Fraser Co.

    Arrangement B
    Finest Glass Co.
    4th Guarantee Bank
    George Fraser Co.
    John O'Farrell Corp.
    Arrangement D
    Finest Glass Co.
    George Fraser Co.
    John O'Farrell Corp.
    4th Guarantee Bank

    10._____

KEY (CORRECT ANSWERS)

1. D
2. B
3. A
4. C
5. B

6. D
7. C
8. A
9. C
10. B

TEST 8

DIRECTIONS: Same as for Test 7.

	Arrangement A	*Arrangement B*	*Arrangement C*	
1.	R. B. Stevens Chas. Stevenson Robert Stevens, Sr. Alfred T. Stevens	Alfred T. Stevens R. B. Stevens Robert Stevens, Sr. Chas. Stevenson	R. B. Stevens Robert Stevens, Sr. Alfred T. Stevens Chas. Stevenson	1._____
2.	Mr. A. T. Breen Dr. Otis C. Breen Amelia K. Brewington John Brewington	John Brewington Amelia K. Brewington Dr. Otis C. Breen Mr. A. T. Breen	Dr. Otis C. Breen Mr. A. T. Breen John Brewington Amelia K. Brewington	2._____
3.	J. Murphy J. J. Murphy John Murphy John J. Murphy	John Murphy John J. Murphy J. Murphy J. J. Murphy	J. Murphy John Murphy J. J. Murphy John J. Murphy	3._____
4.	Anthony DiBuono George Burns, Sr. Geo. T. Burns, Jr. Alan J. Byrnes	Geo. T. Burns, Jr. George Burns, Sr. Anthony DiBuono Alan J. Byrnes	George Burns, Sr. Geo. T. Burns, Jr. Alan J. Byrnes Anthony DiBuono	4._____
5.	James Macauley Frank A. McLowery Francis MacLaughry Bernard J. MacMahon	James Macauley Francis MacLoughry Bernard J. MacMahon Frank A. McLowery	Bernard J. MacMahon Francis MacLaughry Frank A. McLowery James Macauley	5._____
6.	A.J. DiBartolo, Sr. A. P. DiBartolo J. A. Bartolo Anthony J. Bartolo	J. A. Bartolo Anthony J. Bartolo A. P. DiBartolo A. J. DiBartolo, Sr.	Anthony J. Bartolo J. A. Bartolo A. J. DiBartolo, Sr. A. P. DiBartolo	6._____
7.	Edward Holmes Corp. Hillside Trust Corp Standard Insurance Co. The Industrial Surety Co.	Edward Holmes Corp. Hillside Trust Corp. The Industrial Surety Co. Standard Insurance Co.	Hillside TrustCorp. Edward Holmes Corp. The Industrial Surety Co. Standard InsuranceCo.	7._____
8.	Cooperative Credit Co. Chas. Cooke Chemical Corp. John Fuller Baking Co. 4th Avenue Express Co.	Chas. Cooke Chemical Corp. Cooperative Credit Co. 4th Avenue Express Co. John Fuller Baking Co.	4th Avenue Express Co. John Fuller Baking Co. Chas. Cooke Chemical Corp. Cooperative CreditCo.	8._____

2 (#8)

9. Mr. R. McDaniels
Robert Darling, Jr.
F. L. Ramsey
Charles DeRhone

F. L. Ramsey
Mr. R. McDaniels
Charles DeRhone
Robert Darling, Jr.

Robert Darling, Jr. Charles DeRhone
Mr. R. McDaniels
F. L. Ramsey

9._____

10. New York Omnibus Corp.
New York Shipping Co.
Nova Scotia Canning Co.
John J. O'Brien Co.

John J. O'Brien Co.
New York Omnibus Corp.
New York Shipping Co.
Nova Scotia Caning Co.

Nova Scotia Canning Co.
John J. O'Brien Co.
New York Omnibus Corp.
New York Shipping Co.

10._____

KEY (CORRECT ANSWERS)

1. B
2. A
3. A
4. C
5. B

6. C
7. C
8. B
9. C
10. A

TEST 9

DIRECTIONS: Each question consists of a group of names. Consider each group of names as a unit. Determine in what position the name printed in *ITALICS* would be if the names in the group were *CORRECTLY* arranged in alphabetical order. If the name in *ITALICS* should be first, print the letter A; if second, print the letter B; if third, print the letter C; if fourth, print the letter D; and if fifth, print the letter E. *PRINT THE LETTER OF THE CORRECT ANSWER IN THE SPACE AT THE RIGHT.*

SAMPLE QUESTION

J. W. Martin	2
James E. Martin	4
J. Martin	1
George Martins	5
James Martin	3

1. Albert Brown
   James Borenstein
   Frieda Albrecht
   Samuel Brown
   George Appelman

2. James Ryan
   Francis Ryan
   Wm. Roanan
   Frances S. Ryan
   Francis P. Ryan

3. Norman Fitzgibbons
   Charles F. Franklin
   Jas. Fitzgerald
   Andrew Fitzsimmons
   James P. Fitzgerald

4. Hugh F. Martenson
   A. S. Martinson
   Albert Martinsen
   Albert S. Martinson
   M. Martanson

5. Aaron M. Michelson
   Samuel Michels
   Arthur L. Michaelson, Sr.
   John Michell
   Daniel Michelsohn

6. *Chas. R. Connolly*   6.____
    Frank Conlon
    Charles S. Connolly
    Abraham Cohen
    Chas. Conolly

7. James McCormack   7.____
    Ruth MacNamara
    Kathryn McGillicuddy
    Frances Mason
    Arthur MacAdams

8. Dr. Francis Karell   8.____
    John Joseph Karelsen, Jr. John J. Karelsen, Sr.
    Mrs. Jeanette Kelly
    Estelle Karel

9. *The 5th Ave. Bus Co.*   9.____
    The Baltimore and Ohio Railroad
    3rd Ave. Elevated Co.
    Pennsylvania Railroad
    The 4th Ave. Trolley Line

10. Murray B. Cunitz   10.____
    Cunningham Duct Cleaning Corp.
    James A. Cunninghame
    Jason M. Cuomor
    Talmadge L. Cummings

KEY (CORRECT ANSWERS)

1. E
2. D
3. A
4. E
5. D
6. C
7. C
8. D
9. B
10. C

TEST 10

DIRECTIONS: A supervisor who is responsible for the proper maintenance and operation of the filing system in an office of a depart-ment should be able to instruct and guide his subordinates in the correct filing of office records. The following ques-tions,1 through 10, are designed to determine whether you can interpret and follow a prescribed filing procedure. These questions should be answered SOLELY on the basis of the fil-ing instructions which follow.

FILING INSTRUCTIONS FOR PERSONNEL DIVISION DEPARTMENT X

The filing system of this division consists of three separate files, namely: (1) Employee File, (2) Subject File, (3) Correspondence File.

Employee File

This file contains a folder for each person currently employed in the department. Each report, memorandum, and letter which has been received from an official or employee of the department and which pertions to one employee only should be placed in the Employee File folder of the employee with whom the communication is concerned. (Note: This filing proce-dure also applies to a communication from a staff member who writes on a matter which con-cerns himself only.)

Subject File

Reports and memoranda originating in the department and dealing with personnel mat-ters affecting the entire staff or certain categories or groups of employees should be placed in the Subject File under the appropriate subject headings. The materials in this file are subdi-vided under the following five subject headings:

(1) Classification -- includes material on job analysis, change of title, reclassifica-tion of positions, etc.

(2) Employment -- includes material on appointment, promotion, re-instatement, and transfer.

(3) Health and Safety -- includes material dealing chiefly with the health and safety of employees.

(4) Staff Regulations -- includes material pertaining to rules and regulations gov-erning such working conditions as hours of work, lateness, vacation, leave of absence, etc.

(5) Training -- includes all material relating to employee training.

Correspondence File

All correspondence received from outside agencies, both public and private, and from persons outside the department, should be placed in the Correspondence File and cross ref-erenced as follows:

(1) When letters from outside agencies or persons relate to one or more employees currently employed in the department, a cross reference sheet should be placed in the Employee File folder of each employee mentioned.

(2) When letters from outside agencies or persons do not mention a specific employee or specific employees of the department, a cross reference sheet should be placed in the Subject File under the appropriate subject heading.

Questions 1-10 describe communications which have been received and acted upon by the Personnel Division of Department X, and which must be filed in accordance with the Filing Instructions for the Personnel Division.

The following filing operations may be performed in accordance with the above filing instructions:

- (A) Place in Employee File
- (B) Place in Subject File under Classification
- (C) Place in Subject File tinder Employment
- (D) Place in Subject File under Health and Safety
- (E) Place in Subject File under Staff Regulations
- (F) Place in Subject File under Training
- (G) Place in Correspondence File and cross reference in Employee File
- (H) Place in Correspondence File and cross reference in Subject File under Classification
- (I) Place in Correspondence File and cross reference in Subject File under Employment
- (J) Place in Correspondence File and cross reference in Subject File under Health and Safety
- (K) Place in Correspondence File and cross reference in Subject File under Staff Regulations
- (L) Place in Correspondence File and cross reference in Subject File under Training

DIRECTIONS: Examine each of questions 1 through 10 carefully. Then, in the space at the right, *print* the capital letter preceding the one of the filing operations listed above which MOST accurately carries out the Filing Instructions for the Personnel Division.

SAMPLE: A Clerk, Grade 2, in the department has sent in a memorandum requesting information regarding the amount of vacation due him.
The CORRECT answer is A.

1. Mr. Clark, a Clerk, Grade 5, has submitted an intradepartmental memorandum that the titles of all Clerks, Grade 5, in the department be changed to Administrative Assistant. 1.____

2. The secretary to the department has issued a staff order revising the schedule of Saturday work from a one-in-two to a one-in-four schedule. 2.____

3. The personnel officer of another agency has requested the printed transcripts of an in-service course recently conducted by the department. 3.____

4. Mary Smith, a secretary to one of the division chiefs, has sent in a request for a maternity leave of absence to begin on April 1 of this year and to terminate on March 31 of next year. 4.____

5. A letter has been received from a civic organization stating that they would like to know how many employees were promoted in the department during the last fiscal year. 5.____

6. The attorney for a municipal employees' organization has requested permission to represent Mr. James Roe, a departmental employee who is being brought up on charges of violating departmental regulations. 6.____

7. A letter has been received from Mr. Wright, a salesman for a paper company, who complains that Miss Jones, an information clerk in the department, has been rude and impertinent and has refused to give him information which should be available to the public. 7.____

8. Helen Brown, a graduate of Commercial High School, has sent a letter inquiring about an appointment as a provisional typist.   8._____

9. The National Office Managers' Society has sent a request to the department for information on its policies on tardiness and absenteeism.   9._____

10. A memorandum has been received from a division chief who states that employees in his unit have complained that their rest room is in a very unsanitary condition.   10._____

KEY (CORRECT ANSWERS)

1. B
2. E
3. L
4. A
5. I

6. G
7. G
8. I
9. K
10. D

NAME AND NUMBER CHECKING
EXAMINATION SECTION
TEST 1

DIRECTIONS: This test is designed to measure your speed/and accuracy. You are urged to work both quickly and accurately and to do correctly as many lists as you can in the time allowed. The test consists of lists or pairs of names and numbers. Count the number of IDENTICAL pairs in each list. Then, select the correct number, 1, 2, 3, 4, 5, and indicate your choice in the space at the right. Two sample questions are presented for your guidance, together with the correct solutions.

SAMPLE LIST A
Adelphi College – Adelphia College
Braxton Corp – Braxeton Corp.
Wassaic State School – Wassaic State School
Central Islip State Hospital – Central Isllip State Hospital
Greenwich House – Greenwich House

NOTE: There are only two correct pairs—Wassaic State School and Greenwich House. Therefore, the CORRECT answer is 2.

SAMPLE LIST B
78453694 – 78453684
784530 – 784530
533 – 534
67845 – 67845
2368745 – 2368755

NOTE: There are only two correct pairs—784530 and 67845. Therefore, the CORRECT answer is 2.

LIST 1 1.____
 Diagnostic Clinic   – Diagnostic Clinic
 Yorkville Health   – Yorkville Health
 Meinhard Clinic   – Meinhart Clinic
 Corlears Clinic   – Carlears Clinic
 Tremont Diagnostic   – Tremont Diagnostic

LIST 2 2.____
 73526   – 73526
 7283627198   – 7283627198
 627   – 637
 728352617283   – 7283526178282
 6281   – 6281

2 (#1)

LIST 3   3.____
    Jefferson Clinic   – Jeffersen Clinic
    Mott Haven Center   – Mott Havan Center
    Bronx Hospital   – Bronx Hospital
    Montefiore Hospital   – Montifeore Hospital
    Beth Isreal Hospital   – Beth Israel Hospital

LIST 4   4.____
    936271826   – 936371826
    5271   – 5291
    82637192037   – 82637192037
    527182   – 5271882
    726354256   - 72635456

LIST 5   5.____
    Trinity Hospital   – Trinity Hospital
    Central Harlem   – Centrel Harlem
    St. Luke's Hospital   – St. Lukes' Hospital
    Mt. Sinai Hospital   – Mt. Sinia Hospital
    N.Y. Dispensery   – N.Y. Dispensary

LIST 6   6.____
    725361552637   – 725361555637
    7526378   – 7526377
    6975   – 6975
    82637481028   – 82637481028
    3427   – 3429

LIST 7   7.____
    Misericordia Hospital   – Miseracordia Hospital
    Lebonan Hospital   – Lebanon Hospital
    Gouverneur Hospital   – Gouverner Hospital
    German Polyclinic   – German Policlinic
    French Hospital   – French Hospital

LIST 8   8.____
    8277364933251   – 827364933351
    63728   – 63728
    367281   – 367281
    62733846273   – 6273846293
    62836   - 6283

LIST 9   9.____
    King's County Hospital   – Kings County Hospital
    St. Johns Long Island   – St. John's Long Island
    Bellevue Hospital   – Bellvue Hospital
    Beth David Hospital   – Beth David Hospital
    Samaritan Hospital   – Samariton Hospital

3 (#1)

LIST 10   10._____
    62836454   – 62836455
    42738267   – 42738369
    573829   – 573829
    738291627874   – 738291627874
    725   - 735

LIST 11   11._____
    Bloomingdal Clinic   – Bloomingdale Clinic
    Communitty Hospital   – Community Hospital
    Metroplitan Hospital   – Metropoliton Hospital
    Lenox Hill Hospital   – Lonex Hill Hospital
    Lincoln Hospital   – Lincoln Hospital

LIST 12   12._____
    6283364728   – 6283648
    627385   – 627383
    54283902   – 54283602
    63354   – 63354
    7283562781   - 7283562781

LIST 13   13._____
    Sydenham Hospital   – Sydanham Hospital
    Roosevalt Hospital   – Roosevelt Hospital
    Vanderbilt Clinic   – Vanderbild Clinic
    Women's Hospital   – Woman's Hospital
    Flushing Hospital   – Flushing Hospital

LIST 14   14._____
    62738   – 62738
    727355542321   – 72735542321
    263849332   – 263849332
    262837   – 263837
    47382912   - 47382922

LIST 15   15._____
    Episcopal Hospital   – Episcapal Hospital
    Flower Hospital   – Flouer Hospital
    Stuyvesent Clinic   – Stuyvesant Clinic
    Jamaica Clinic   – Jamaica Clinic
    Ridgwood Clinic   – Ridgewood Clinic

LIST 16   16._____
    628367299   – 628367399
    111   – 111
    118293304829   – 1182839489
    4448   – 4448
    333693678   - 333693678

4 (#1)

LIST 17   17._____
    Arietta Crane Farm   – Areitta Crane Farm
    Bikur Chilim Home   – Bikur Chilom Home
    Burke Foundation   – Burke Foundation
    Blythedale Home   – Blythdale Home
    Campbell Cottages   – Cambell Cottages

LIST 18   18._____
    32123   – 32132
    273893326783   – 27389326783
    473829   – 473829
    7382937   – 7383937
    3628890122332   - 36289012332

LIST 19   19._____
    Caraline Rest   – Caroline Rest
    Loreto Rest   – Loretto Rest
    Edgewater Creche   – Edgwater Creche
    Holiday Farm   – Holiday Farm
    House of St. Giles   – House of st. Giles

LIST 20   20._____
    557286777   – 55728677
    3678902   – 3678892
    1567839   – 1567839
    7865434712   – 7865344712
    9927382   - 9927382

LIST 21   21._____
    Isabella Home   – Isabela Home
    James A. Moore Home   – James A. More Home
    The Robin's Nest   – The Roben's Nest
    Pelham Home   – Pelam Home
    St. Eleanora's Home   – St. Eleanora's Home

LIST 22   22._____
    273648293048   – 273648293048
    334   – 334
    7362536478   – 7362536478
    7362819273   – 7362819273
    7362   - 7363

LIST 23   23._____
    St. Pheobe's Mission   – St. Phebe's Mission
    Seaside Home   – Seaside Home
    Speedwell Society   – Speedwell Society
    Valeria Home   – Valera Home
    Wiltwyck   - Wildwyck

LIST 24
- 63728 – 63738
- 63728192736 – 63728192738
- 428 – 458
- 62738291527 – 62738291529
- 63728192 - 63728192

24.____

LIST 25
- McGaffin – McGafin
- David Ardslee – David Ardslee
- Axton Supply – Axeton Supply Co
- Alice Russell – Alice Russell
- Dobson Mfg. Co. – Dobsen Mfg. Co.

25.____

KEY (CORRECT ANSWERS)

1.	3	11.	1
2.	3	12.	2
3.	1	13.	1
4.	1	14.	2
5.	1	15.	1
6.	2	16.	3
7.	1	17.	1
8.	2	18.	1
9.	1	19.	1
10.	2	20.	2

21.	1
22.	4
23.	2
24.	1
25.	2

TEST 2

DIRECTIONS: This test is designed to measure your speed/and accuracy. You are urged to work both quickly and accurately and to do correctly as many lists as you can in the time allowed. The test consists of lists or pairs of names and numbers. Count the number of IDENTICAL pairs in each list. Then, select the correct number, 1, 2, 3, 4, 5, and indicate your choice in the space at the right.

LIST 1 1.____
    82637381028 — 82637281028
    928 — 928
    72937281028 — 72937281028
    7362 — 7362
    927382615 — 927382615

LIST 2 2.____
    Albee Theatre — Albee Theatre
    Lapland Lumber Co. — Laplund Lumber Co.
    Adelphi College — Adelphi College
    Jones & Son Inc. — Jones & Sons Inc.
    S.W. Ponds Co. — S.W. Ponds Co.

LIST 3 3.____
    85345 — 85345
    895643278 — 895643277
    726352 — 726353
    632685 — 632685
    7263524 — 7236524

LIST 4 4.____
    Eagle Library — Eagle Library
    Dodge Ltd. — Dodge Co.
    Stromberg Carlson — Stromberg Carlsen
    Clairice Ling — Clairice Linng
    Mason Book Co. — Matson Book Co.

LIST 5 5.____
    66273 — 66273
    629 — 629
    7382517283 — 7382517283
    637281 — 639281
    2738261 — 2788261

LIST 6 6.____
    Robert MacColl — Robert McColl
    Buick Motor — Buck Motors
    Murray Bay & Co. Ltd. — Murray Bay Co. Ltd.
    L.T. Ltyle — L.T. Lyttle
    A.S. Landas — A.S. Landas

LIST 7
    6271526374890   − 627152637490
    73526189   − 73526189
    5372   − 5392
    637281142   − 63728124
    4783946   − 4783046

7.____

LIST 8
    Tyndall Burke   − Tyndell Burke
    W. Briehl   − W. Briehl
    Burritt Publishing Co.   − Buritt Publishing Co.
    Frederick Breyer & Co.   − Frederick Breyer Co.
    Bailey Buulard   − Bailey Bullard

8.____

LIST 9
    634   − 634
    16837   − 163837
    273892223678   − 27389223678
    527182   − 527782
    3628901223   − 3629002223

9.____

LIST 10
    Ernest Boas   − Ernest Boas
    Rankin Barne   − Rankin Barnes
    Edward Appley   − Edward Appely
    Camel   − Camel
    Caiger Food Co.   − Caiger Food Co.

10.____

LIST 11
    6273   − 6273
    322   − 332
    15672839   − 15672839
    63728192637   − 63728192639
    738   − 738

11.____

LIST 12
    Wells Fargo Co.   − Wells Fargo Co.
    W.D. Brett   − W.D. Britt
    Tassco Co.   − Tassko Co.
    Republic Mills   − Republic Mill
    R.W. Burnham   − R.W. Burhnam

12.____

LIST 13
    7253529152   − 7283529152
    6283   − 6383
    52839102738   − 5283910238
    308   − 398
    82637201927   − 8263720127

13.____

LIST 14
Schumacker Co.	– Shumacker Co.	14._____
C.H. Caiger	– C.H. Caiger	
Abraham Strauss	– Abram Straus	
B.F. Boettjer	– B.F. Boettijer	
Cut-Rate Store	– Cut-Rate Stores	

LIST 15
15273826	– 15273826	15._____
72537	– 73537	
726391027384	– 62639107384	
637389	– 627399	
725382910	– 725382910	

LIST 16
Hixby Ltd.	– Hixby Lt'd.	16._____
S. Reiner	– S. Riener	
Reynard Co.	– Reynord Co.	
Esso Gassoline Co.	– Esso Gasolene Co.	
Belle Brock	– Belle Brock	

LIST 17
7245	– 7245	17._____
819263728192	– 819263728172	
682537289	– 682537298	
789	– 789	
82936542891	– 82936542891	

LIST 18
Joseph Cartwright	– Joseph Cartwrite	18._____
Foote Food Co.	– Foot Food Co.	
Weiman & Held	– Weiman & Held	
Sanderson Shoe Co.	– Sandersen Shoe Co.	
A.M. Byrne	– A.N. Byrne	

LIST 19
4738267	– 4738277	19._____
63728	– 63729	
6283628901	– 6283628991	
918264	– 918264	
263728192037	– 2637728192073	

LIST 20
Exray Laboratories	– Exray Labratories	20._____
Curley Toy Co.	– Curly Toy Co.	
J. Lauer & Cross	– J. Laeur & Cross	
Mireco Brands	– Mireco Brands	
Sandor Lorand	– Sandor Larand	

4 (#2)

LIST 21   21.____
   607   – 609
   6405   – 6403
   976   – 996
   101267   – 101267
   2065432   – 20965432

LIST 22   22.____
   John Macy & Sons   – John Macy & Son
   Venus Pencil Co.   – Venus Pencil Co.
   Nell McGinnis   – Nell McGinnis
   McCutcheon & Co.   – McCutcheon & Co.
   Sun-Tan Oil   – Sun-Tan Oil

LIST 23   23.____
   703345700   – 703345700
   46754   – 466754
   3367490   – 3367490
   3379   – 3778
   47384   – 47394

LIST 24   24.____
   arthritis   – arthritis
   asthma   – asthma
   endocrine   – endocrene
   gastro-enterological – gastrol-enteralogical
   orthopedic   – orthopedic

LIST 25   25.____
   743829432   – 743828432
   998   – 998
   732816253902   – 732816252902
   46829   – 46830
   7439120249   – 7439210249

KEY (CORRECT ANSWERS)

1.	4	11.	3
2.	3	12.	1
3.	2	13.	1
4.	1	14.	1
5.	2	15.	2
6.	1	16.	1
7.	2	17.	3
8.	1	18.	1
9.	1	19.	1
10.	3	20.	1

21. 1
22. 4
23. 2
24. 3
25. 1

CODING

COMMENTARY

An ingenious question-type called coding, involving elements of alphabetizing, filing, name and number comparison, and evaluative judgment and application, has currently won wide acceptance in testing circles for measuring clerical aptitude and general ability, particularly on the senior (middle) grades (levels).

While the directions for this question usually vary in detail, the candidate is generally asked to consider groups of names, codes, and numbers, and, then, according to a given plan, to arrange codes in alphabetic order; to arrange these in numerical sequence; to re-arrange columns of names and numbers in correct order; to espy errors in coding; to choose the correct coding arrangement in consonance with the given directions and examples, etc.

This question-type appears to have few paramaters in respect to form, substance, or degree of difficulty.

Accordingly, acquaintance with, and practice in, the coding question is recommended for the serious candidate.

EXAMINATION SECTION
TEST 1

DIRECTIONS:

CODE TABLE

Name of Applicant	H	A	N	G	S	B	R	U	K	E
Test Code	c	o	m	p	l	e	x	i	t	y
File Number	0	1	2	3	4	5	6	7	8	9

Assume that each of the above *capital letters* is the first letter of the Name of an Applicant, that the *small letter* directly beneath each capital letter is the Test Code for the Applicant, and that the *number* directly beneath each code letter is the File Number for the Applicant.

In each of the following questions, the test code letters and the file numbers in Columns 2 and 3 should correspond to the capital letters in Column 1. For each question, look at each column carefully and mark your answer as follows:

If there is an error only in Column 2, mark your answer A.
If there is an error only in Column 3, mark your answer B.
If there is an error in both Columns 2 and 3, mark your answer C.
If both Columns 2 and 3 are correct, mark your answer D.

The following sample question is given to help you understand the procedure.

SAMPLE QUESTION

Column 1	Column 2	Column 3
AKEHN	otyci	18902

2 (#1)

In Column 2, the final test code letter "i" should be "m." Column 3 is correctly coded to Column 1. Since there is an error only in Column 2, the answer is A

	Column 1	Column 2	Column 3	
1.	NEKKU	mytti	29987	1. ___
2.	KRAEB	txlye	86095	2. ___
3.	ENAUK	ymoit	92178	3. ___
4.	REANA	xeomo	69121	4. ___
5.	EKHSE	ytcxy	97049	5. ___

KEY (CORRECT ANSWERS)

1. B
2. C
3. D
4. A
5. C

TEST 2

DIRECTIONS: The employee identification codes in Column I begin and end with a capital letter and have an eight-digit number in between. In Questions 1 through 8, employee identification codes in Column I are to be arranged according to the following rules:

First: Arrange in alphabetical order according to the first letter.

Second: When two or more employee identification codes have the same first letter, arrange in alphabetical order according to the last letter.

Third: When two or more employee codes have the same first and last letters, arrange in numerical order beginning with the lowest number.

The employee identification codes in Column I are numbered 1 through 5 in the order in which they are listed. In Column II the numbers 1 through 5 are arranged in four different ways to show different arrangements of the corresponding employee identification numbers. Choose the answer in Column II in which the employee identification numbers are arranged according to the above rules.

SAMPLE QUESTION

Column I
1. E75044127B
2. B96399104A
3. B93939086A
4. B47064465H
5. B99040922A

Column II
A. 4, 1, 3, 2, 5
B. 4, 1, 2, 3, 5
C. 4, 3, 2, 5, 1
D. 3, 2, 5, 4, 1

In the sample question, the four employee identification codes starting with B should be put before the employee identification code starting with E. The employee identification codes starting with B and ending with A should be put before the employee identification codes starting with B and ending with H. The three employee identification codes starting with B and ending with A should be listed in numerical order, beginning with the lowest number. The correct way to arrange the employee identification codes, therefore, is 3, 2, 5, 4, 1 shown below.

3. B93939086A
2. B96399104A
5. B99040922A
4. B47064465H
1. E75044127B

Therefore, the answer to the sample question is D. Now answer the following questions according to the above rules.

Column I

1.
   1. G42786441J
   2. H45665413J
   3. G43117690J
   4. G43546698I
   5. G41679942I

Column II

A. 2, 5, 4, 3, 1
B. 5, 4, 1, 3, 2
C. 4, 5, 1, 3, 2
D. 1, 3, 5, 4, 2

1.____

2.	1. S44556178T	A. 1, 3, 5, 2, 4	2.___
	2. T43457169T	B. 4, 3, 5, 2, 1	
	3. S53321176T	C. 5, 3, 1, 2, 4	
	4. T53317998S	D. 5, 1, 3, 4, 2	
	5. S67673942S		

3.
   1. R63394217D
   2. R63931247D
   3. R53931247D
   4. R66874239D
   4. R46799366D

   A. 5, 4, 2, 3, 1
   B. 1, 5, 3, 2, 4
   C. 5, 3, 1, 2, 4
   D. 5, 1, 2, 3, 4

   3.___

4.
   1. A35671968B
   2. A35421794C
   3. A35466987B
   4. C10435779A
   5. C00634779B

   A. 3, 2, 1, 4, 5
   B. 2, 3, 1, 5, 4
   C. 1, 3, 2, 4, 5
   D. 3, 1, 2, 4, 5

   4.___

5.
   1. I99746426Q
   2. I10445311Q
   3. J63749877P
   4. J03421739Q
   5. J00765311Q

   A. 2, 1, 3, 5, 4
   B. 5, 4, 2, 1, 3
   C. 4, 5, 3, 2, 1
   D. 2, 1, 4, 5, 3

   5.___

6.
   1. M33964217N
   2. N33942770N
   3. N06155881M
   4. M00433669M
   5. M79034577N

   A. 4, 1, 5, 2, 3
   B. 5, 1, 4, 3, 2
   C. 4, 1, 5, 3, 2
   D. 1, 4, 5, 2, 3

   6.___

7.
   1. D77643905C
   2. D44106788C
   3. D13976022F
   4. D97655430E
   5. D00439776F

   A. 1, 2, 5, 3, 4
   B. 5, 3, 2, 1, 4
   C. 2, 1, 5, 3, 4
   D. 2, 1, 4, 5, 3

   7.___

8.
   1. W22746920A
   2. W22743720A
   3. W32987655A
   4. W43298765A
   5. W30987433A

   A. 2, 1, 3, 4, 5
   B. 2, 1, 5, 3, 4
   C. 1, 2, 3, 4, 5
   D. 1, 2, 5, 3, 4

   8.___

KEY (CORRECT ANSWERS)

1.	B	5.	A
2.	D	6.	C
3.	C	7.	D
4.	D	8.	B

TEST 3

DIRECTIONS: Each of the following equations consists of three sets of names and name codes. In each question, the two names and name codes on the same line are supposed to be exactly the same.

Look carefully at each set of names and codes and mark your answer:
- A. if there are mistakes in all three sets
- B. if there are mistakes in two of the sets
- C. if there is a mistake in only one set
- D. if there are no mistakes in any of the sets

The following sample question is given to help you understand the procedure.

Macabe, John N. - V	53162	Macade, John N. - V	53162
Howard, Joan S. - J	24791	Howard, Joan S. - J	24791
Ware, Susan B. - A	45068	Ware, Susan B. - A	45968

In the above sample question, the names and name codes of the first set are not exactly the same because of the spelling of the last name (Macabe - Macade). The names and name codes of the second set are exactly the same. The names and name codes of the third set are not exactly the same because the two name codes are different (A 45068 - A 45968), Since there are mistakes in only 2 of the sets, the answer to the sample question is B.

1. Powell, Michael C. - 78537 F   Powell, Michael C. - 78537 F   1.____
   Martinez, Pablo, J. - 24435 P   Martinez, Pablo J. - 24435 P
   MacBane, Eliot M. - 98674 E   MacBane, Eliot M. - 98674 E

2. Fitz-Kramer Machines Inc. - 259090 Fitz-Kramer Machines Inc. - 259090   2.____
   Marvel Cleaning Service - 482657   Marvel Cleaning Service - 482657
   Donate, Carl G. - 637418   Danato, Carl G. - 687418

3. Martin Davison Trading Corp. - 43108 T   Martin Davidson Trading Corp. - 43108 T   3.____
   Cotwald Lighting Fixtures - 76065 L   Cotwald Lighting Fixtures - 70056 L
   R. Crawford Plumbers - 23157 C   R. Crawford Plumbers - 23157 G

4. Fraiman Engineering Corp. - M4773   Friaman Engineering Corp. -M4773   4.____
   Neuman, Walter B. - N7745   Neumen, Walter B. - N7745
   Pierce, Eric M. - W6304   Pierce, Eric M. - W6304

5. Constable, Eugene - B 64837   Comstable, Eugene - B 64837   5.____
   Derrick, Paul - H 27119   Derrik, Paul - H 27119
   Heller, Karen - S 49606   Heller, Karen - S 46906

6. Hernando Delivery Service Co. - D 7456   Hernando Delivery Service Co. - D 7456   6.____
   Barettz Electrical Supplies - N 5392   Barettz Electrical Supplies - N 5392
   Tanner, Abraham - M 4798   Tanner, Abraham - M 4798

7. Kalin Associates - R 38641   Kaline Associates - R 38641   7.____
   Sealey, Robert E. - P 63533   Sealey, Robert E. - P 63553
   Scalsi Office Furniture   Scalsi Office Furniture

2 (#3)

8. Janowsky, Philip M.- 742213
    Hansen, Thomas H. - 934816
    L. Lester and Son Inc. - 294568

    Janowsky, Philip M.- 742213
    Hanson, Thomas H. - 934816
    L. Lester and Son Inc. - 294568

8.____

KEY (CORRECT ANSWERS)

1. D
2. C
3. A
4. B
5. A

6. D
7. B
8. C

TEST 4

DIRECTIONS: The following questions are to be answered on the basis of the following Code Table. In this table, for each number, a corresponding code letter is given. Each of the questions contains three pairs of numbers and code letters. In each pair, the code letters should correspond with the numbers in accordance with the Code Table.

CODE TABLE

Number	1	2	3	4	5	6	7	8	9	0
Corresponding Code Letter	Y	N	Z	X	W	T	U	P	S	R

In some of the pairs below, an error exists in the coding. Examine the pairs in each question carefully. If an error exists in:
- Only one of the pairs in the question, mark your answer A.
- Any two pairs in the question, mark your answer B.
- All three pairs in the question, mark your answer C.
- None of the pairs in the question, mark your answer D.

SAMPLE QUESTION

37258 - ZUNWP
948764 - SXPTTX
73196 - UZYSP

In the above sample, the first pair is correct since each number, as listed, has the correct corresponding code letter. In the second pair, an error exists because the number 7 should have the code letter U instead of the letter T. In the third pair, an error exists because the number 6 should have the code letter T instead of the letter P. Since there are errors in two of the three pairs, the correct answer is B.

1. 493785 - XSZUPW
   86398207 - PTUSPNRU
   5943162 - WSXZYTN

2. 5413968412 - WXYZSTPXYR
   8763451297 - PUTZXWYZSU
   4781965302 - XUPYSUWZRN

3. 79137584 - USYRUWPX
   638247 - TZPNXS
   49679312 - XSTUSZYN

4. 37854296 - ZUPWXNST
   09183298 - RSYXZNSP
   91762358 - SYUTNXWP

5. 3918762485 - ZSYPUTNXPW
   1578291436 - YWUPNSYXZT
   2791385674 - NUSYZPWTUX

121

6. 197546821 - YSUWSTPNY
   873024867 - PUZRNWPTU
   583179246 - WPZYURNXT

   6._____

7. 510782463 - WYRUSNXTZ
   478192356 - XUPYSNZWT
   961728532 - STYUNPWXN

   7._____

KEY (CORRECT ANSWERS)

1. A
2. C
3. B
4. B
5. D
6. C
7. B

TEST 5

DIRECTIONS: Assume that each of the capital letters is the first letter of the name of a city using EAM equipment. The number directly beneath each capital letter is the code number for the city. The small letter beneath each code number is the code letter for the number of EAM divisions in the city and the + or - symbol directly beneath each code letter is the code symbol which signifies whether or not the city uses third generation computers with the EAM equipment.

The questions that follow show City Letters in Column I, Code Numbers in Column II, Code Letters in Column III, and Code Symbols in Column IV. If correct, each City Letter in Column I should correspond by position with each of the three codes shown in the other three columns, in accordance with the coding key shown. BUT there are some errors. For each question,

If there is a total of ONE error in Columns 2, 3, and 4, mark your answer A.
If there is a total of TWO errors in Columns 2, 3, and 4, mark your answer B.
If there is a total of THREE errors in Columns 2, 3, and 4, mark your answer C.
If Columns 2, 3, and 4 are correct, mark your answer D.

SAMPLE QUESTION

I	II	III	IV
City Letter	Code Numbers	Code Letters	Code Symbols
Y J M O S	5 3 7 9 8	e b g i h	- - + + -

The errors are as follows: In Column 2, the Code Number should be "2" instead of "3" for City Letter "J," and in Column 4 the Code Symbol should be "+" instead of "-" for City Letter "Y." Since there is a total of two errors in Columns 2, 3, and 4, the answer to this sample question is B.

Now answer questions 1 through 9 according to these rules.

```
                    CODING KEY
        City  Letter      P  J  R  T  Y  K  M  S  O
        Code  Number      1  2  3  4  5  6  7  8  9
        Code  Letter      a  b  c  d  e  f  g  h  i
        Code  Symbol      +  -  +  -  +  -  +  -  +
```

	I City Letters	II Code Numbers	III Code Letters	IV Code Symbols	
1.	K O R M P	6 9 3 7 1	f i e g a	- - + + +	1._____
2.	O T P S Y	9 4 1 8 6	b d a h e	+ - - - +	2._____
3.	R S J T M	3 8 1 4 7	c h b e g	- - - - +	3._____
4.	P M S K J	1 7 8 6 2	a g h f b	+ + - - -	4._____
5.	M Y T J R	7 5 4 2 3	g e d f c	+ + - - +	5._____
6.	T P K Y O	4 1 6 7 9	d a f e i	- + - + -	6._____
7.	S K O R T	8 6 9 3 5	h f i c d	- - + + -	7._____
8.	J R Y P K	2 3 5 1 9	b d e a f	- + + + -	8._____
9.	R O M P Y	4 9 7 1 5	c i g a d	+ + - + +	9._____

123

KEY (CORRECT ANSWERS)

1. B
2. C
3. C
4. D
5. A

6. B
7. A
8. B
9. C

TEST 6

Assume that each of the capital letters is the first letter of the name of an offense, that the small letter directly beneath each capital letter is the code letter for the offense, and that the number directly beneath each code letter is the file number for the offense.

DIRECTIONS: In each of the following questions, the code letters and file numbers should correspond to the capital letters.

If there is an error only in Column 2, mark your answer A.
If there is an error only in Column 3, mark your answer B.
If there is an error in both Column 2 and Column 3, mark your answer C.
If both Columns 2 and 3 are correct, mark your answer D.

SAMPLE QUESTION

Column 1	Column 2	Column 3
BNARGHSVVU	emoxtylcci	6357905118

The code letters in Column 2 are correct but the first "5" in Column 3 should be "2." Therefore, the answer is B. Now answer the following questions according to the above rules.

CODE TABLE

Name of Offense	V	A	N	D	S	B	R	U	G	H
Code Letter	c	o	m	p	l	e	x	i	t	y
File Number	1	2	3	4	5	6	7	8	9	0

	Column 1	Column 2	Column 3	
1.	HGDSBNBSVR	ytplxmelcx	0945736517	1.____
2.	SDGUUNHVAH	lptiimycoy	5498830120	2.____
3.	BRSNAAVUDU	exlmooctpi	6753221848	3.____
4.	VSRUDNADUS	cleipmopil	1568432485	4.____
5.	NDSHVRBUAG	mplycxeiot	3450175829	5.____
6.	GHUSNVBRDA	tyilmcexpo	9085316742	6.____
7.	DBSHVURANG	pesycixomt	4650187239	7.____
8.	RHNNASBDGU	xymnolepti	7033256398	8.____

KEY (CORRECT ANSWERS)

1. C
2. D
3. A
4. C
5. B

6. D
7. A
8. C

TEST 7

DIRECTIONS: Each of the following questions contains three sets of code letters and code numbers. In each set, the code numbers should correspond with the code letters as given in the Table, but there is a coding error in some of the sets. Examine the sets in each question carefully.

Mark your answer A if there is a coding error in only *ONE* of the sets in the question.
Mark your answer B if there is a coding error in any *TWO* of the sets in the question.
Mark your answer C if there is a coding error in all *THREE* sets in the question.
Mark your answer D if there is a coding error in *NONE* of the sets in the question.

SAMPLE QUESTION

fgzduwaf - 35720843
uabsdgfw - 04262538
hhfaudgs - 99340257

In the above sample question, the first set is right because each code number matches the code letter as in the Code Table. In the second set, the corresponding number for the code letter b is wrong because it should be 1 instead of 2. In the third set, the corresponding number for the last code letter s is wrong because it should be 6 instead of 7. Since there is an error in two of the sets, the answer to the above sample question is B.

In the Code Table below, each code letter has a corresponding code number directly beneath it.

CODE TABLE

Code Letter	b	d	f	a	g	s	z	w	h	u
Code Number	1	2	3	4	5	6	7	8	9	0

1. fsbughwz - 36104987   zwubgasz - 78025467   1.____
   ghgufddb - 59583221

2. hafgdaas - 94351446   ddsfabsd - 22734162   2.____
   wgdbssgf - 85216553

3. abfbssbd - 41316712   ghzfaubs - 59734017   3.____
   sdbzfwza - 62173874

4. whfbdzag - 89412745   daaszuub - 24467001   4.____
   uzhfwssd - 07936623

5. zbadgbuh - 71425109   dzadbbsz - 27421167   5.____
   gazhwaff - 54798433

6. fbfuadsh - 31304265   gzfuwzsb - 57300671   6.____
   bashhgag - 14699535

KEY (CORRECT ANSWERS)

1. B
2. C
3. B
4. B
5. D
6. C

TEST 8

DIRECTIONS: The following questions are to be answered on the basis of the following Code Table. In this table every letter has a corresponding code number to be punched. Each question contains three pairs of letters and code numbers. In each pair, the code numbers should correspond with the letters in accordance with the Code Table.

CODE TABLE

Letter	P	L	A	N	D	C	O	B	U	R
Corresponding Code Number	1	2	3	4	5	6	7	8	9	0

In some of the pairs below, an error exists in the coding. Examine the pairs in each question. Mark your answer

- A if there is a mistake in only *one* of the pairs
- B if there is a mistake in only *two* of the pairs
- C if there is a mistake in *all three* of the pairs
- D if there is a mistake in *none* of the pairs

SAMPLE QUESTION

LCBPUPAB - 26819138
ACOABOL - 3683872
NDURONUC - 46901496

In the above sample, the first pair is correct since each letter as listed has the correct corresponding code number. In the second pair, an error exists because the letter O should have the code number 7, instead of 8. In the third pair, an error exists because the letter D should have the code number 5, instead of 6. Since there are errors in two of the three pairs, your answer should be B.

1. ADCANPLC - 35635126   DORURBBO - 57090877   1.____
   PNACBUCP - 14368061

2. LCOBLRAP - 26782931   UPANUPCD - 91349156   2.____
   RLDACLRO - 02536207

3. LCOROPAR - 26707130   BALANRUP - 83234091   3.____
   DOPOAULL - 57173922

4. ONCRUBAP - 74609831   DCLANORD - 56243705   4.____
   AORPDUR - 3771590

5. PANRBUCD - 13408965   UAOCDPLR - 93765120   5.____
   OPDDOBRA - 71556803

6. BAROLDCP - 83072561   PNOCOBLA - 14767823   6.____
   BURPDOLA - 89015723

7. ANNCPABO - 34461387   DBALDRCP - 58325061   7.____
   ACRPOUL - 3601792

2 (#8)

8. BLAPOUR - 8321790   NOACNPL - 4736412   8. _____
   RODACORD - 07536805

9. ADUBURCL - 3598062   NOCOBAPR - 47578310   9. _____
   PRONDALU - 10754329

10. UBADCLOR - 98356270   NBUPPARA - 48911033   10. _____
    LONDUPRC - 27459106

KEY (CORRECT ANSWERS)

1. C
2. B
3. D
4. B
5. A
6. D
7. B
8. B
9. C
10. A

TEST 9

DIRECTIONS: Answer questions 1 through 10 ONLY on the basis of the following information.

Column I consists of serial numbers of dollar bills. Column II shows different ways of arranging the corresponding serial numbers.

The serial numbers of dollar bills in Column I begin and end with a capital letter and have an eight-digit number in between. The serial numbers in Column I are to be arranged according to the following rules:

FIRST: In alphabetical order according to the first letter.

SECOND: When two or more serial numbers have the same first letter, in alphabetical order according to the last letter.

THIRD: When two or more serial numbers have the same first and last letters, in numerical order, beginning with the lowest number.

The serial numbers in Column I are numbered (1) through (5) in the order in which they are listed. In Column II the numbers (1) through (5) are arranged in four different ways to show different arrangements of the corresponding serial numbers. Choose the answer in Column II in which the serial numbers are arranged according to the above rules.

SAMPLE QUESTION

	COLUMN I	COLUMN II
(1)	E75044127B	(A) 4, 1, 3, 2, 5
(2)	B96399104A	(B) 4, 1, 2, 3, 5
(3)	B93939086A	(C) 4, 3, 2, 5, 1
(4)	B47064465H	(D) 3, 2, 5, 4, 1
(5)	B99040922A	

In the sample question, the four serial numbers starting with B should be put before the serial number starting with E. The serial numbers starting with B and ending with A should be put before the serial number starting with B and ending with H. The three serial numbers starting with B and ending with A should be listed in numerical order, beginning with the lowest number. The correct way to arrange the serial numbers, therefore, is:

(3) B93939086A
(2) B96399104A
(5) B99040922A
(4) B47064465H
(1) E75044127B

Since the order of arrangement is 3, 2, 5, 4, 1, the answer to the sample question is (D).

	COLUMN I		COLUMN II
1. (1)	P44343314Y	A.	2, 3, 1, 4, 5
(2)	P44141341S	B.	1, 5, 3, 2, 4
(3)	P44141431L	C.	4, 2, 3, 5, 1
(4)	P41143413W	D.	5, 3, 2, 4, 1
(5)	P44313433H		
2. (1)	D89077275M	A.	3, 2, 5, 4, 1
(2)	D98073724N	B.	1, 4, 3, 2, 5
(3)	D90877274N	C.	4, 1, 5, 2, 3
(4)	D98877275M	D.	1, 3, 2, 5, 4
(5)	D98873725N		

2 (#9)

3.	(1)	H32548137E	A.	2,	4,	5,	1,	3
	(2)	H35243178A	B.	1,	5,	2,	3,	4
	(3)	H35284378F	C.	1,	5,	2,	4,	3
	(4)	H35288337A	D.	2,	1,	5,	3,	4
	(5)	H32883173B						
4.	(1)	K24165039H	A.	4,	2,	5,	3,	1
	(2)	F24106599A	B.	2,	3,	4,	1,	5
	(3)	L21406639G	C.	4,	2,	5,	1,	3
	(4)	C24156093A	D.	1,	3,	4,	5,	2
	(5)	K24165593D						
5.	(1)	H79110642E	A.	2,	1,	3,	5,	4
	(2)	H79101928E	B.	2,	1,	4,	5,	3
	(3)	A79111567F	C.	3,	5,	2,	1,	4
	(4)	H79111796E	D.	4,	3,	5,	1,	2
	(5)	A79111618F						
6.	(1)	P16388385W	A.	3,	4,	5,	2,	1
	(2)	R16388335V	B.	2,	3,	4,	5,	1
	(3)	P16383835W	C.	2,	4,	3,	1,	5
	(4)	R18386865V	D.	3,	1,	5,	2,	4
	(5)	P18686865W						
7.	(1)	B42271749G	A.	4,	1,	5,	2,	3
	(2)	B42271779G	B.	4,	1,	2,	5,	3
	(3)	E43217779G	C.	1,	2,	4,	5,	3
	(4)	B42874119C	D.	5,	3,	1,	2,	4
	(5)	E42817749G						
8.	(1)	M57906455S	A.	4,	1,	5,	3,	2
	(2)	N87077758S	B.	3,	4,	1,	5,	2
	(3)	N87707757B	C.	4,	1,	5,	2,	3
	(4)	M57877759B	D.	1,	5,	3,	2,	4
	(5)	M57906555S						
9.	(1)	C69336894Y	A.	2,	5,	3,	1,	4
	(2)	C69336684V	B.	3,	2,	5,	1,	4
	(3)	C69366887W	C.	3,	1,	4,	5,	2
	(4)	C69366994Y	D.	2,	5,	1,	3,	4
	(5)	C69336865V						
10.	(1)	A56247181D	A.	1,	5,	3,	2,	4
	(2)	A56272128P	B.	3,	1,	5,	2,	4
	(3)	H56247128D	C.	3,	2,	1,	5,	4
	(4)	H56272288P	D.	1,	5,	2,	3,	4
	(5)	A56247188D						

KEY (CORRECT ANSWERS)

1. D   6. D
2. B   7. B
3. A   8. A
4. C   9. A
5. C   10. D

TEST 10

DIRECTIONS: Answer the following questions on the basis of the instructions, the code, and the sample questions given below. Assume that an officer at a certain location is equipped with a two-way radio to keep him in constant touch with his security headquarters. Radio messages and replies are given in code form, as follows:

CODE TABLE

Radio Code for Situation	J	P	M	F	B
Radio Code for Action to be Taken	o	r	a	z	q
Radio Response for Action Being Taken	1	2	3	4	5

Assume that each of the above capital letters is the radio code for a particular type of situation, that the small letter below each capital letter is the radio code for the action an officer is directed to take, and that the number directly below each small letter is the radio response an officer should make to indicate what action was actually taken.

In each of the following questions, the code letter for the action directed (Column 2) and the code number for the action taken (Column 3) should correspond to the capital letters in Column 1.

INSTRUCTIONS: If only Column 2 is different from Column 1, mark your answer I.
If only Column 3 is different from Column 1, mark your answer II.
If both Column 2 and Column 3 are different from Column 1, mark your answer III.
If both Columns 2 and 3 are the same as Column 1, mark your answer IV.

SAMPLE QUESTION

Column 1	Column 2	Column 3
JPFMB	orzaq	12453

The CORRECT answer is: A. I B. II C. III D. IV

The code letters in Column 2 are correct, but the numbers "53" in Column 3 should be "35." Therefore, the answer is B. Now answe the following questions according to the above rules.

	Column 1	Column 2	Column 3	
1.	PBFJM	rqzoa	25413	1.____
2.	MPFBJ	zrqao	32541	2.____
3.	JBFPM	oqzra	15432	3.____
4.	BJPMF	qaroz	51234	4.____
5.	PJFMB	rozaq	21435	5.____
6.	FJBMP	zoqra	41532	6.____

KEY (CORRECT ANSWERS)

1. D
2. C
3. B
4. A
5. D
6. A

ARITHMETICAL REASONING
EXAMINATION SECTION
TEST 1

DIRECTIONS: Each question or incomplete statement is followed by several suggested answers or completions. Select the one that BEST answers the question or completes the statement. *PRINT THE LETTER OF THE CORRECT ANSWER IN THE SPACE AT THE RIGHT.*

1. In 2015, a public agency spent $180 to buy pencils that cost three cents each. In 2017, the agency spent $420 to buy the same number of pencils that it had bought in 2015.
   The price per pencil that the agency paid in 2017 was _____ cents.
   A. 6⅓   B. ⅔   C. 7   D. 7¾

2. A stenographer spent her 35 hour work week on taking dictation, transcribing the dictate material, and filing.
   If she spent 20% of the work week on taking dictation and ½ of the remaining time on transcribing the dictated material, the number of hours of the work week that she spent on filing was
   A. 7   B. 10.5   C. 14   D. 17.4

3. A typist typed eight pages in two hours.
   If she typed an average of 50 lines per page and an average of 12 words per line, what was her typing speed, in words per minute?
   A. 40   B. 50   C. 60   D. 80

4. The daily compensation to be paid to each consultant hired in a certain agency is computed by dividing his professional earnings in the previous year by 250. The maximum daily compensation they can receive is $200 each. Four consultants who were hired to work on a special project had the following professional earnings in the previous year: $37,500, $144,000, $46,500, and $61,100.
   What will be the TOTAL daily cost to the agency for these four consultants?
   A. $932   B. $824   C. $736   D. $712

5. In a typing and stenographic pool consisting of 30 employees, 2/5 of them are typists, 1/3 of them are senior typists and senior stenographers, and the rest are stenographers.
   If there are 5 more stenographers than senior stenographers, how many senior stenographers are in the typing and stenographic pool?
   A. 3   B. 5   C. 8   D. 10

6. There are 3,330 copies of a three-page report to be collated. One clerk starts collating at 9:00 A.M. and is joined 15 minutes later by two other clerks. It takes 15 minutes for each of these clerks to collate 90 copies of the report. At what time should the job be completed if all three clerks continue working at the same rate without breaks?
   A. 12:00 Noon   B. 12:15 P.M.   C. 1:00 P.M.   D. 1:15 P.M.

7. By the end of last year, membership in the blood credit program in a certain agency had increased from the year before by 500, bringing the total to 2,500. If the membership increased by the same percentage this year, the TOTAL number of members in the blood credit program for this agency by the end of this year should be
   A. 2,625   B. 3,000   C. 3,125   D. 3,250

8. During this year, an agency suggestion program put into practice suggestions from 24 employee, thereby saving the agency 40 times the amount of money it paid in awards.
   If $1/3$ of the employees were awarded $50 each, ½ of the employees were awarded $25 each, and the rest were awarded $10 each, how much money did the agency save by using the suggestions?
   A. $18,760   B. $29,600   C. $32,400   D. $46,740

9. A senior stenographer earned $20,100 a year and had 4.5% state tax withheld for the year.
   If she was paid every two weeks, the amount of state tax that was taken out of each of her paychecks, based on a 52-week year, was MOST NEARLY
   A. $31.38   B. $32.49   C. $34.77   D. $36.99

10. Two stenographers have been assigned to address 750 envelopes. One stenographer addresses twice as many envelopes per hour as the other stenographer.
    If it takes five hours for them to complete the job, the rate of the slower stenographer is _____ envelopes per hour.
    A. 35   B. 50   C. 75   D. 100

11. Suppose that the postage rate for mailing single copies of a magazine to persons not included on a subscription list is 18 cents for the first two ounces of the single copy and 3 cents for each additional ounce.
    Of 19 copies of a magazine, each of which weighs eleven ounces, are mailed to 19 different people, the TOTAL postage cost of these magazines is
    A. $3.42   B. $3.99   C. $6.18   D. $8.55

12. A senior stenographer spends about 40 hours a month taking dictation. Of that time, 44% is spent taking minutes of meetings, 38% if spent taking dictation of lengthy reports, and the rest of the time is spent taking dictation of letters and memoranda.
    How much more time is spent taking minutes of meetings than n taking dictation of letters and memoranda? 10 hours _____ minutes.
    A. 6   B. 16   C. 24   D. 40

13. In one week, a stenographer typed 65 letter. Forty letters had 4 copies on colored paper. The rest had 3 copies on colored paper.
If the stenographer had 50 sheets of colored paper on hand at the beginning of the week when she started typing the letters, how many sheets of colored paper did she have left at the end of the week?
A. 190 B. 235 C. 265 D. 305

14. An agency is planning to microfilm letters and other correspondence of the last five years. The number of letter-size documents that can be photographed on a 100-foot roll of microfilm is 2,995. The agency estimates that it will need 240 feet of microfilm to do all the pages of all of the letters.
How many pages of letter-size documents can be photographed on this microfilm?
A. 5,990 B. 6,785 C. 7,188 D. 7,985

15. In an agency, $2/3$ of the total number of female stenographers and ½ of the total number of male stenographers attended a general staff meeting.
If there are a total of 56 stenographers in the agency and 25% of them are male, the number of female stenographers who attended the general staff meeting is
A. 14 B. 28 C. 36 D. 42

16. A worker is currently earning $17,140 a year and pays $350 a month for rent. He expects to get a raise that will enable him to move into an apartment where his rent will be 25% of his new yearly salary.
If this new apartment is going to cost him $390 a month, what is the TOTAL amount of raise that he expects to get?
A. $480 B. $980 C. $1,580 D. $1,840

17. The tops of five desks in an office are to be covered with a scratch-resistant material. Each desk top measures 60 inches by 36 inches.
How many square feet of material will be needed for the five desk tops?
A. 15 B. 75 C. 96 D. 180

18. Three grades of bond paper are used in a central transcribing unit. The cost per ream of paper is $1.90 for Grade A, $1.70 for Grade B, and $1.60 for Grade C.
If the central transcribing unit used 6 reams of Grade A paper, 14 reams of Grade B paper, and 20 reams of Grade C paper, the AVERAGE cost, per ream, of the bond paper used by this unit is between
A. $1.62 and $1.66
B. $1.66 and $1.70
C. $1.70 and $1.74
D. $1.73 and $1.80

19. The Complaint Bureau of a city agency is composed of an investigation unit, a clerical unit, and a central transcribing unit. The sum of $264,000 has been appropriated for the operation of this bureau. Of this sum, $170,000 is to be allotted to the clerical unit.

Of this bureau's total appropriation, the percentage that is left for the central transcribing unit is MOST NEARLY _____ if 41,200 is allotted for investigations.
A. 20% B. 30% C. 40% D. 50%

20. Three typists were assigned to address a total of 2,655 postcards. Typist A addressed postcards at the rate of 170 per hour. Typist B addressed the postcards at the rate of 150 per hour. Typist C's rate is not known. After the three typists had addressed postcards for three and a half hours, Typist C was taken off this assignment. It was necessary for Typist A and Typist B to work two and a half hours more to complete this assignment. The rate per hour at which Typist C addressed the postcards was
A. less than 150
B. between 150 and 170
C. more than 170 but less than 200
D. more than 200

21. In 2015, a city agency bought 12,000 envelopes at $4.00 per hundred. In 2016, the price of envelopes purchased was 40 percent higher than the 2010 price, but only 60 percent as many envelopes were bought.
The total cost of the envelopes purchased in 2016 was MOST NEARLY
A. $250 B. $320 C. $400 D. $480

22. A stenographer has been assigned to place entries on 500 forms. She places entries on 25 forms by the end of half an hour, when she is joined by another stenographer. The second stenographer places entries at the rate of 45 an hour.
Assuming both stenographers continue to work at their respective rates of speed, the TOTAL number of hours required to carry out the entire assignment is
A. 5 B. 5¼ C. 6¼ D. 7

23. On Monday, a stenographer took dictation without interruption for 1½ hours and transcribed all the dictated material in 3½ hours. On Tuesday, she took dictation uninterruptedly for 1¾ hours and transcribed all the material in 3¾ hours. On Wednesday, she took dictation without interruption for 2¼ hours and transcribed all the material in 4½ hours.
If she took dictation at the average rate of 90 words per minute during these three days, then her average transcription rate, in words per minute, for the same three days was MOST NEARLY
A. 36 B. 41 C. 54 D. 58

24. In a division of clerks and stenographers, 15 people are currently employed, 20% of whom are stenographers.
If management plans are to maintain the current number of stenographers, but to increase the clerical staff to the point where 12% of the total staff are stenographers, what is the MAXIMUM number of additional clerks that should be hired to meet these plans?
A. 3 B. 8 C. 10 D. 12

25. In the first quarter of the year, a certain operator sent out 230 quarterly reports. 25._____
In the second quarter of that year, he sent out 310 quarterly reports.
The percent increase in the number of quarterly reports he sent out in the
second quarter of the year compared to the first quarter of the year is MOST
NEARLY
   A. 26% B. 29% C. 35% D. 39%

KEY (CORRECT ANSWERS)

1.	C	11.	D
2.	C	12.	C
3.	A	13.	C
4.	C	14.	C
5.	A	15.	B
6.	B	16.	C
7.	C	17.	B
8.	B	18.	B
9.	C	19.	A
10.	B	20.	D

21.	C
22.	B
23.	B
24.	C
25.	C

SOLUTIONS TO PROBLEMS

1. $180 ÷ .03 = 6000 pencils bought. In 2017, the price per pencil = $420/6000 = .07 = 7 cents

2. Number of hours on filing = 35 − (.20)(35) · (½)(28) = 14

3. Eight pages contain (8)(50)(12) = 4800 words. She thus typed 4800 words in 120 minutes = 40 words per minute

4. $37,500 ÷ 250 = $150; $144,000 ÷ 250 = $576; $46,500 ÷ 250 = $186; $61,100 ÷ 250 = $244.40. Since $200 = maximum compensation for any single consultant, total compensation = $150 + $200 + $186 + $200 = $736

5. Number of typists = (2/5)(30) = 12, number of senior typists and senior stenographers = ($1/3$)(30) = 10, number of stenographers = 30 − 12 − 10 = 8. Finally, number of senior stenographers = 8 − 5 = 3

6. At 9:15 A.M., 90 copies have been collated. The remaining 3,240 copies are being collated at the rate of (3)(90) = 270 every 15 minutes = 1080 per hour. Since 3240 ÷ 1080 = 3 hours, the clerks will finish at 9:15 A.M. + 3 hours = 12:15 P.M.

7. During the last year, the membership increased from 2000 to 2500, which represents a (500/2000)(100) = 25% increase. A 25% increase during this year means the membership = (2500)(1.25) = 3125

8. Total awards = ($1/3$)(24)($50) + (½)(24)($25) + ($1/6$)(24)($10) = $740. Thus, the savings = (40)($740) = $29,600

9. Her pay for 2 weeks = $20,100 ÷ 26 ≈ $773.08. Thus, her state tax for 2 weeks = ($773.08)(.045) ≈ $34.79. (Nearest correct answer is $34.77 in four selections.)

10. 750 ÷ 5 hours = 150 envelopes per hour for the 2 stenographers combined. Let x = number of envelopes addressed by the slower stenographer. Then, x + 2x = 150. Solving, = 50

11. Total cost = (19)[.18+(.03)(9)] = $8.55

12. (.44)(40) − (.18)(40) = 10.4 hours = 10 hrs. 24 min.

13. 500 − (40)(4) − (25)(3) = 265

14. 2995 ÷ 100 = 29.95 documents per foot of microfilm roll. Then, (29.95)(240 ft) = 7188 documents

15. There are (.75)(56) = 42 female stenographers. Then, ($2/3$)(42) = 28 of them attended the meeting

7 (#1)

16. ($390)(12) = $4679 new rent per year. Then, ($4680)(4) = $18,720 = his new yearly salary. His raise = $18,720 - $17,140 = $1580

17. Number of sq. ft. = (5)(60)(36) ÷ 144 = 75

18. Average cost per ream = [(1.90)(6) + ($1.70)(14) + ($1.60)(20)] /40 = $1.68, which is between $1.66 and $1.77

19. $264,000 - $170,000 - $41,200 = 52,800 = 20%

20. Let x = typist C's rate. Since Typists A and B each worked 6 hrs., while Typist C worked only 3.5 hours, we have (6)(170) + (6)(150) + 3.5x = 2655. Solving, x = 210, which is mre than 200

21. In 2016, the cost per hundred envelopes was ($4.00)(1.40) = $5.60 and (.60)(12,000) = 7200 envelopes were bought. Total cost in 2016 = (72)($5.60) = $403.20, or about $400

22. The first stenographer's rate is 50 forms per hour. After ½ hour, there are 500 – 25 = 475 forms to be done and the combined rate of the 2 stenographers is 95 forms per hr. Thus, total hours required = ½ + (475) ÷ (95) = 5½

23. Total time for dictation = 1¼ + 1¾ + 2¼ = 5¼ hrs. = 315 min. The number of words = (90)(315) = 28,350. The total transcription 3 time = 3¼ + 3¾ + 44 = 11½ hrs. = 690 min. Her average transcription rate = 28,350 ÷ 690 ≈ 41 words per min.

24. Currently, there are (.20)(15) = 3 stenographers, and thus 12 clerks. Let x = additional clerks. Then, $\frac{3}{3+12+x}$ = .12. This simplifies to 3 = (.12)(15+x). Solving, x = 10

25. Percent increase = $(\frac{80}{230})$(100) ≈ 35%

TEST 2

DIRECTIONS: Each question or incomplete statement is followed by several suggested answers or completions. Select the one that BEST answers the question or completes the statement. *PRINT THE LETTER OF THE CORRECT ANSWER IN THE SPACE AT THE RIGHT.*

1. A school has 112 homeroom classes. There were 15 school days in February. The aggregate register of the school for the month of February was 52,920; the aggregate attendance was 43,860.
   The average class size, to the NEAREST tenth, is
   A. 35.3   B. 31.5   C. 29.2   D. 26.9

   1.____

2. As the school secretary in charge of supplies, you are asked to order the following items on a supplementary requisition for general supplies:
       5 gross of red pencils at $8.90 per dozen
       5,000 manila envelopes at $2.35 per C
       36 rulers at $187.20 per gross
       6 boxes of manila paper at $307.20 per carton (24 boxes to a carton)
       180 reams of composition paper at $27.80 per carton (20 reams to a carton)
   The TOTAL amount of the order is
   A. $957.20   B. $1,025.30   C. $916.80   D. $991.30

   2.____

3. In the high school to which you have been assigned as a school secretary, the annual allotment for general supplies, textbooks, repairs, etc. for the school year 2015-16 was $37,500. A special allotment of $10,000 was granted for textbooks ordered from the State Textbook List. The original requisition for general and vocational supplies amounted to $12,514.75; for science supplies, $6,287.75; for textbooks, including the special funds, $13,785.00; monies spent for equipment repairs and science perishables through December 31, 2015, $1,389.68.
   The balance in your supply allotment account on January 1, 2016 will be
   A. $14,913.00   B. $13,523.32   C. $17,308.32   D. $3,523.32

   3.____

4. The teacher of one of the sixth term typing classes in the high school to which you are assigned as a school secretary has agreed to have her students type attendance cards for the incoming students for the new schoolyear, commencing in September, as a work project. There are 24 students in the class; each student can complete 8 cards during a typing period. There will be 4,032 new students in September.
   The number of typing periods required to complete the task is
   A. 31   B. 21   C. 28   D. 24

   4.____

5. As a school secretary assigned to payroll duties, you are required to prepare the extra-curricular payroll report for the coaches teams in your high school. The rate of pay for these activities was increased on November 1 from $148 per session to $174.50 per session. The pay period which you are reporting is for the months of October, November, and December. Mr. Jones, the football coach, conducted 15 practice sessions in October, 20 in November, and 30 in December.

   5.____

142

His TOTAL gross pay on the December extra-curricular payroll report is
A. $10,547.50   B. $10,415.00   C. $10,945.00   D. $11,342.50

6. The comparative results on a uniform examination given in your school for the last three years follow:

	2014	2015	2016
Number Taking Test	501	496	485
Number Passing Test	441	437	436

The percentage of passing, to the nearest tenth of a percent, for the year in which the HIGHEST percent of students passed is
A. 89.3%   B. 88%   C. 89.9%   D. 90.3%

7. During his first seven terms in high school, a student compiled the following averages:

Term	Numbers of Majors Completed	Average
1	4	81.25%
2	4	83.75%
3	5	86.2%
4	5	85.8%
5	5	87.0%
6	5	83.4%
7	5	82.6%

In his eighth term, the student had the following final marks in major subjects: 90%, 95%, 80%, 90%, 85%. The student's average for all eight terms of high school, correct to the nearest tenth of a percent, is
A. 84.8%   B. 84.7%   C. 84.9%   D. 85.8%

8. A secretary is asked by her employer to order an office machine which lists at a price of $360, less trade discounts of 20% and 10%, terms 2/10, n/30. There is a delivery charge of $8 and an installation charge of $12.
If the machine is paid for in 10 days, the TOTAL cost of the machine will be
A. $264.80   B. $258.40   C. $266.96   D. $274.02

9. The school to which you have been assigned as school secretary has an annual allowance of 5,120 hours for all teacher aides. The principal decides to employ 5 teacher aides from 8:00 A.M. to 12:00 Noon, and 5 other teacher aides from 12:00 Noon to 4:00 P.M. daily for as many days as his allowance permits.
If a teacher aide earns $17.00 an hour, and he is present every day, his TOTAL earnings for the school year will be more than
A. $7,000 but less than $8,000   B. $8,000 but less than $9,000
C. $9,000 but less than $10,000   D. $10,000

3 (#2)

10. During examination week in a high school to which you have been assigned as school secretary, teachers are required to be in school at least 6 hours and 20 minutes daily although their arrival and departure times may vary each day. A teacher's time card that you have been asked to check shows the following entries for the week of June 17:

Date	Arrival	Departure
17	7:56 A.M.	2:18 P.M.
18	9:54 A.M.	4:22 P.M.
19	12:54 P.M.	7:03 P.M.
20	9:51 A.M.	4:15 P.M.
21	7:58 A.M.	2:11 P.M.

During the week of June 17 to June 21, the teacher was in school for AT LEAST the minimum required time on _____ days.
   A. 2 of the 5   B. 3 of the 5   C. 4 of the 5   D. all 5

10._____

11. As school secretary, you are asked to find the total of the following bill received in your school:
    750 yellow envelopes at $.22 per C
    2,400 white envelopes at $2.80 per M
    30 rulers at $5.04 per gross
The TOTAL of the bill is
   A. $69.90   B $24.27   C. $18.87   D. $9.42

11._____

12. A department in the school to which you have been assigned as school secretary has been given a textbook allowance of $5,50 for the school year. The department's textbook order is:
    75 books at $32.50 each
    45 books at $49.50 each
    25 books at $34.50 each
The TOTAL of the department's order is _____ the allowance.
   A. $27.50 over   B. $27.50 under
   C. $72.50 under   D. $57.50 over

12._____

13. The total receipts, including 5% city sales tax, for the G.O. store for the first week of school amounted to $489.09.
The receipts from the G.O. store for the first week of school, excluding the 5% city sales tax, amounted to
   A. $465.89   B. $364.64   C. $464.63   D. $513.54

13._____

14. Class sizes in the school to which you have been assigned as school secretary are as follows:

Number of Classes	Class Size
9	29
12	31
15	32
7	33
11	34

14._____

The average class size in this school, correct to the nearest tenth, is
A. 30.8   B. 31.9   C. 31.8   D. 30.9

15. In 2013, the social security tax was 4.2% for the first $6,600 earned a year. In 2014, the social security tax was 4.4% on the first $6,600 earned a year. For a teacher aide earning $19,200 in 2013 and $20,400 in 2014, the increase in social security tax deduction in 2014 over 2013 was
A. $132.00   B. $13.20   C. $19.20   D. $20.40

15.____

16. A teacher aide earning $23,900 a year will incur automatic deductions of 3.90% for social security and .50% for Medicare, based on the first $6,600 a year earnings.
The TOTAL deduction for these two items will be
A. $274   B. $290.40   C. $525.80   D. $300.40

16.____

17. The school store turns in receipts totaling $131.25 to the school treasurer, including 5% which has been collected for sales tax.
The amount of money which the treasurer MUST set aside for sales tax is
A. $6.56   B. $6.25   C. $5.00   D. $5.25

17.____

18. One of the custodial assistants can wash all the windows in the main office in 3 hours. A second assistant can wash the windows in the main office in 2 hours.
If the two men work together, they should complete the task in _____ hour(s) _____ minutes.
A. 1; 0   B. 1.5; 0   C. 1; 12   D. 1; 15

18.____

19. A school secretary is requested by the principal to order an office machine which lists at a price of $120, less discounts of 10% and 5%.
The net price of the machine to the school will be
A. $100.50   B. $102.00   C. $102.60   D. $103.00

19.____

20. Five students are employed at school under a work-study program through which they are paid $10.00 an hour for work in school offices, but no student may earn more than $450 a month. Three days before the end of the month, you note that the student payroll totals $2,062.50.
The number of hours which each of the students may work during the remainder of the month is _____ hour(s).
A. 4   B. 2   C. 1   D. 3

20.____

21. You are asked to summarize expenditures made by the school within the budget allocation for the school year. You determine that the following expenditures have been made: educational supplies, $2,600; postage, $650; emergency repairs, $225; textbooks, $5,100; instructional equipment, $1,200. Since $10,680 has been allocated to the school, the following sum still remains available for office supplies.
A. $905   B. $1,005   C. $800   D. $755

21.____

5 (#2)

22. In preparing the percentage of attendance for the period report, you note that the aggregate attendance is 57,585 and the aggregate register is 62,000.
The percentage of attendance, to the nearest tenth of a percent, is
A. 91.9%   B. 93.0%   C. 92.8%   D. 92.9%

22.____

23. You borrow $1,200 from your retirement fund which you must repay over a period of three years, with interest of $144, each payment to be divided equally among 36 total payments.
The monthly deduction from your paycheck will be
A. $37.33   B. $36.00   C. $33.00   D. $37.30

23.____

24. Tickets for a school dance are printed, starting with number 401 and ending with number 1650. They are to be sold for $7.50 each. The tickets remaining unsold should start with number 1569.
The amount of cash which should be collected for the sale of tickets is
A. $876.75   B. $937.50   C. $876.00   D. $875.25

24.____

25. Stage curtains are purchased by the school and delivered on October 3 under terms of 5/10, 2/30, net/60. The curtains are paid in full by a check for $522.50 on October 12.
The invoice price was
A. $533.16   B. $522.50   C. $540.00   D. $550.00

25.____

KEY (CORRECT ANSWERS)

1.	B		11.	D
2.	B		12.	A
3.	B		13.	A
4.	B		14.	C
5.	C		15.	B
6.	C		16.	B
7.	C		17.	B
8.	D		18.	C
9.	B		19.	C
10.	B		20.	D

21. A
22. D
23. A
24. C
25. D

SOLUTIONS TO PROBLEMS

1. Average class size = 52,920 ÷ 15 ÷ 112 = 31.5

2. Total amount = (5)(12)($8.90) + (50)($2.35) + (36)($187.20) ÷ 144 + (6)($307.20) ÷ 24 + (9)($27.80) = $1,025.30

3. Balance = $37,500 + $10,000 - $12,514.75 - $6,287.25 - $13,785 - $1,389.68 = $13,523.32

4. (24)(8) = 192 cards completed in one period. Then, 4032 ÷ 192 = 21 typing periods required

5. Total pay = (15)($148.00) + (20)($174.50) + (30)($174.50) = $10,945.00

6. The passing rates for 2014, 2015, and 2016 were 88.0%, 88.1%, and 89.9%, respectively. So, 89.9% was the highest

7. His 8th term average was 88.0%. His overall average for all 8 terms = [(4)(81.25%) + (4)(83.75%) + (5)(86.2%) + (5)(85.8%) + (5)(87.0%) + (5)(83.4%) + (5)(82.6%) + (5)(88.0%)] ÷ 38 = 84.9%

8. Total cost = ($360)(.80)(.90)(.98) + $8 + $12 ≈ $274.02 (Exact amount = $274.016)

9. 5120 ÷ 4 = 1280 teacher-days. Then, 1280 ÷ 20 = 128 days per teacher. A teacher's earnings for these 128 days = ($17.00)(4)(128) = $8,704, which is more than $8,000 but less than $9,000

10. The number of hours present on each of the 5 days listed was 6 hrs. 22 min., 6 hrs. 29 min., 6 hrs. 9 min., 6 hrs. 24 min., and 6 hrs. 13 min. On 3 days, he met the minimum time.

11. Total cost = (7.5)(.22) + (2.4)($2.80) + (30/144)(5.04) = $9.42

12. Textbook order = (75)($32.50) + (45)($49.50) + (25)($34.50) = $5,527.5, which is $27.50 over the allowance

13. Receipts without the tax = $489.09 ÷ 1.05 = $465.80

14. Average class size = [(9)(29) + (12)(31) + (7)(33) + (15)(32)] ÷ 54 ≈ 31.8

15. ($6,600)(.044-.042) = $13.20

16. ($6,600)(.039+.005) = $290.40

17. $131.25 = 1.05x, x = 125, $131.25 – 125.00 = 6.25

18. Let x = hours needed working together. Then, $(1/3)(x) + (1/2)(x) = 1$
    Simplifying, $2x + 3x = 6$. Solving, $x = 1^1/_5$ hrs. = 1 hr. 12 min.

19. Net price = 120 – 10% (12) = 108; 108 – 5% (5.40) = 102.60

20. ($225)(5) - $1031.25 = $93.75 remaining in the month. Since the 5 students earn $25 per hour combined, $93.75 ÷ $25 = 3.75, which must be rounded down to 3 hours

21. $10,680 - $2,600 - $650 - $225 - $5,100 - $1,200 = $905 for office supplies

22. 57,585 ÷ 62,000 ≈ .9288 ≈ 92.9%

23. Monthly deduction = $1344 ÷ 36 = $37.33. (Technically, 35 payments of $37.33 and 1 payment of $37.45)

24. (1569-401) = $876.00

25. The invoice price (which reflects the 5% discount) is $522.50 ÷ .95 = $550.00

TEST 3

DIRECTIONS: Each question or incomplete statement is followed by several suggested answers or completions. Select the one that BEST answers the question or completes the statement. *PRINT THE LETTER OF THE CORRECT ANSWER IN THE SPACE AT THE RIGHT.*

1. If an inch on an office layout drawing equals 4 feet of actual floor dimension, then a room which actually measures 9 feet by 14 feet is represented on the drawing by measurements equaling _____ inches × _____ inches.
   A. 2¼; 3½ B. 2½; 3½ C. 2¼; 3¼ D. 2½; 3¼

   1.____

2. A cooperative education intern works from 1:30 P.M. to 5 P.M. on Mondays, Wednesdays, and Fridays, and from 10 A.M. to 2:30 P.M. with no lunch hour on Tuesdays and Thursdays. He earns $13.50 an hour on this job. In addition, he has a Saturday job paying $16.00 an hour at which he works from 9 A.M. to 3 P.M. with a half hour off for lunch.
   The gross amount that the student earns each week is MOST NEARLY
   A. $321.90 B. $355.62 C. $364.02 D. $396.30

   2.____

3. Thirty-five percent of the College Discovery students who entered community college earned an associate degree. Of these students, 89% entered senior college, of which 67% went on to earn baccalaureate degrees.
   If there were 529 College Discovery students who entered community college, then the number of those who went on to finally receive a baccalaureate degree is MOST NEARLY
   A. 354 B. 315 C. 124 D. 110

   3.____

4. It takes 5 office assistants two days to type 125 letters. Each of the assistants works at an equal rate of speed.
   How many days will it take 10 office assistants to type 200 letters?
   A. 1 B. 1³/₅ C. 2 D. 2¹/₅

   4.____

5. The following are the grades and credits earned by Student X during the first two years in college.

Grade	Credits	Weight	Quality Points
A	10 ½	×4	
B	24	×3	
C	12	×2	
D	4 ½	×1	
F, FW	5	×0	

   To compute an index number:
   I. Multiply the number of credits of each grade by the weight to get the number of quality points
   II. Add the credits
   III. Add the quality points
   IV. Divide the total quality point by the total credits and carry the division to two decimal places

   5.____

149

On the basis of the given information, the index number for Student X is
A. 2.55   B. 2.59   C. 2.63   D. 2.68

6. Typist X can type 20 forms per hour, and Typist Y can type 30 forms per hour. If there are 30 forms to be typed and both typists are put to work on the job, how son should they be expected to finish the work?
_____ minutes.
A. 32   B. 34   C. 36   D. 38

7. Assume that there were 18 working days in February and that the six clerks in your unit had the following number of absences:

Clerk	Absences
F	3
G	2
H	8
I	1
J	0
K	5

The average percentage attendance for the six clerks in your unit in February was MOST NEARLY
A. 80%   B. 82%   C. 84%   D. 86%

8. A certain employee is paid at the rate of $7.50 per hour, with time and a half for overtime. Hours in excess of 40 hours a week count as overtime. During the past week, the employee put in 48 working hours.
The employee's gross wages for the week are MOST NEARLY
A. $330   B. $350   C. $370   D. $390

9. You are making a report on the number of inside and outside calls handled by a particular switchboard. Over a 15-day period, the total number of all inside and outside calls handled by the switchboard was 5,760. The average number of inside calls per day was 234. You cannot find one day's tally of outside calls, but the total number of outside calls for the other fourteen days was 2,065.
From this information, how many outside calls must have been reported on the missing tally?
A. 175   B. 185   C. 195   D. 205

10. A floor plan has been prepared for a new building, drawn to a scale of ¾ inch = 1 foot. A certain area is drawn 1 and ½ feet long and 6 inches wide on the floor plan.
What are the ACTUAL dimensions of this area in the new building?
_____ feet long and _____ feet wide
A. 21; 8   B. 24; 8   C. 27; 9   D. 30; 9

11. You are preparing a package of six books to mail to a professor who is on sabbatical. They weigh, respectively, 1 pound 11 ounces, 1 pound 6 ounces, 2 pounds 1 ounce, 2 pounds 2 ounces, 1 pound 7 ounces, and 1 pound 8 ounces. The packaging material weighs 6 ounces.
The TOTAL weight of the package will be _____ pounds _____ ounces.
    A. 10; 3   B. 10; 9   C. 11; 5   D. 12; 5

11._____

12. Part-time students are charged $70 per credit for courses at a particular college. In addition, they musts pay a $24.00 student activity fee if they take six credits or more and $14.00 lab fee for each laboratory course.
If a person takes one 3-credit course and one 4-credit course and his 4-credit course is a laboratory course, the TOTAL cost to him will be
    A. $504   B. $528   C. $542   D. $552

12._____

13. The graduating course of a certain community college consisted of 378 majors in secretarial science, 265 majors in engineering science, 57 majors in nursing, 513 majors in accounting, and 865 majors in liberal arts.
The percent of students who major in liberal arts at this college was MOST NEARLY
    A. 24.0%   B. 41.6%   C. 52.3%   D. 71.6%

13._____

14. Donald Smith earns $12.80 an hour for forty hours a week, with time and a half for all hours over forty. Last week, his total earnings amounted to $627.20.
He worked _____ hours.
    A. 46   B. 47   C. 48   D. 49

14._____

15. Mr. Jones desires to sell an article costing $28 at a gross profit of 30% of the selling price, and to allow a trade discount of 20% of the list price.
The list price of the article should be
    A. $43.68   B. $45.50   C. $48.00   D. $50.00

15._____

16. The gauge of an oil storage tank in an elementary school indicates 1/5 full. After a truck delivers 945 gallons of oil, the gauge indicates 4/5 full.
The capacity of the tank is _____ gallons.
    A. 1,260   B. 1,575   C. 1,625   D. 1,890

16._____

17. An invoice dated April 3, terms 3/10, 2/30, net/60, was paid in full with a check for $787.92 on May 1.
The amount of the invoice was
    A. $772.16   B. $787.92   C. $804.00   D. $812.29

17._____

18. Two pipes supply the water for the swimming pool at Blenheim High School. One pipe can fill the pool in 9 hours. The second pipe can fill the pool in 6 hours.
If both pipes were opened simultaneously, the pool could be filled in _____ hours _____ minutes.
    A. 3; 36   B. 4; 30   C. 5; 15   D. 7; 30

18._____

19. John's father spent $24,000, which was one-fourth of his savings. He bought a car with three-eighths of the remainder of his savings.
His bank balance now amounts to
A. $30,000   B. $32,000   C. $45,000   D. $50,000

20. A clock that loses 4 minutes every 24 hours was set at 6 A.M. on October 1 What time was indicated by the clock when the CORRECT time was 12:00 Noon on October 6th?
A. 11:36   B. 11:38   C. $11:39   D. 11:40

21. Unit S's production fluctuated substantially from one year to another. In 2009, Unit s's production was 100% greater than in 2008. In 2010, production decreased by 25% from 2009. In 2011, Unit S's production was 10% greater than in 2010.
On the basis of this information, it is CORRECT to conclude that Unit S's production in 2011 exceeded Unit S's production in 2008 by
A. 65%   B. 85%   C. 95%   D. 135%

22. Agency X is moving into a new building. It has 1,500 employees presently on its staff and does not contemplate much variance from this level. The new building contains 100 available offices, each with a maximum capacity of 30 employees. It has been decided that only 2/3 of the maximum capacity of each office will be utilized.
The TOTAL number of office that will be occupied by Agency X is
A. 30   B. 65   C. 75   D. 90

23. One typist completes a form letter every 5 minutes and another typist completes one every 6 minutes.
If the two typists start together, how many minutes later will they again start typing new letters simultaneously and how many letters will they have completed by that time?
A. 11; 30   B. 12; 24   C. 24; 12   D. 30; 1

24. During one week, a machine operator produces 10 fewer pages per hour of work than he usually does.
If it ordinarily takes him six hours to produce a 300-page report, how many hour LONGER will that same 300-page report take him during the week when he produces more slowly?
A. 1½   B. 1²/₃   C. 2   D. 2¾

25. A study reveals that Miss Brown files N cards in M hours, and Miss Smith files the same number of cards in T hours.
If the two employees work together, the number of hours it will take them to file N cards is
A. $\dfrac{N}{\frac{N}{M}+\frac{N}{N}}$ B. $\dfrac{N}{T+M}+\dfrac{2N}{MT}$ C. $N(\dfrac{M}{N}+\dfrac{N}{T})$ D. $\dfrac{N}{NT+MN}$

KEY (CORRECT ANSWERS)

1. A
2. B
3. D
4. B
5. A

6. C
7. B
8. D
9. B
10. B

11. B
12. B
13. B
14. A
15. D

16. B
17. C
18. A
19. C
20. C

21. A
22. C
23. D
24. A
25. A

6 (#3)

SOLUTIONS TO PROBLEMS

1. 9/4 = 2¼" and 14/4 = 3½"

2. Gross amount = (3)($6.75)(3.5) + (2)($6.75)(4.5) + ($8.00)(5.5) = $174.624, which is closest to selection B ($177.81)

3. (529)(.35)(.89)(.67) ≈ 110

4. 10 worker-days are needed to type 125 letters, so (200)(10) ÷ 125 = 16 worker-days are needed to type 200 letters. Finally, 16 ÷ 10 workers = 1 3/5 days

5. Index number = [(14)(10½) + (3)(24) + (2)(12) + (1)(4½) + (0)(5)] ÷ 56 ≈ 2,54

6. Typist X could do 30 forms in 30/20 = 1½ hours. Let x = number of hour needed when working together with Typist Y.
   Then, $(\frac{1}{1\frac{1}{2}})(x) + (\frac{1}{1})x = 1$. Simplifying, 2x + 3x = 3, so x = $\frac{3}{5}$ hr. = 36 min.

7. (3+2+8+1+0+5) ÷ 6 = 3.16. Then, 18 − 3.$\overline{6}$ = 14.$\overline{83}$.

   Finally, 14.8$\overline{3}$ ÷ 18 ≈ 82%

8. Wages = ($7.50)(40) + ($11.25)(8) = $390

9. (234)(15) = 3510 inside calls. Then, 5760 − 3510 = 2259 outside calls. Finally, 2250 − 2065 = 185 outside calls on the missing day.

10. 18 ÷ ¾ - 24 feet long and 6 ÷ ¾ = 8 feet wide

11. Total weight = 1 lb. 11 oz. + 1 lb. 6 oz. + 2 lbs. 1 oz. + 2 lbs. 2 oz. + 1 lb. 7 oz. + 1 lb. 8 oz. + 6 oz = 8 lbs. 41 oz. 10 lbs. 9 oz.

12. Total cost = ($70)(7) + $24 + $14 = $528

13. 865 ÷ 2078 ≈ 41.6% liberal arts majors

14. ($12.80)(40) = $512, so he made $627.20 - $512 = $115.20 in overtime. His overtime rate = ($12.80)(1.5) = $19.20 per hour. Thus, he worked $115.20 ÷ $19.20 = 6 overtime hours. Total hours worked = 46

15. Let x = list price. Selling price = .80x. Then, .80x − (.30)(.80x) = $28. Simplifying, .56x = $28. Solving, x = $50.00

7 (#3)

16. 945 gallons represents $\frac{4}{5} \cdot \frac{1}{5} = \frac{3}{5}$ of the tank's capacity.

    Then, the capacity = $945 \div \frac{3}{5}$ = 1575 gallons

17. $787.92 ÷ .98 = $804.00

18. Let x = number of required hours. Then, (1/9)(x) + (1/6)(x) = 1
    Simplifying, 2x + 3x = 18. Solving, x = 3.6 hours = 3 hours 36 minutes

19. Bank balance = $96,000 - $24,000 – (3/8)($72,000) = $45,000

20. From Oct. 1, 6 A.M. to Oct. 6, Noon = 5½ days. The clock would show a loss of (4 min.)(5½) = 21 min. Thus, the clock's time would incorrectly) show 12:00 Noon – 21 min. = 11:39 A.M.

21. 2008 = x, 2009 = 200x, 2010 = 150x, 2011 = 165x
    65% more

22. (2/3)(30) = 20 employees in each office. Then, 1500 ÷ 20 = 75 offices

23. After 30 minutes, the typists will have finished a total of 6 + 5 = 11 letters

24. When he works more slowly, he will only produce 300 – (6)(10) = 240 pages in 6 hrs. His new slower rate is 40 pages per hour, so he will need 60/40 = 1½ more hours to do the remaining 60 pages.

25. Let x = required hours. Then $(\frac{1}{M})(x) + (\frac{1}{10})(x) = 1$.

    Simplifying, x(T+M) = MT. Solving, x = MT/(T+M)

    Note: The N value is immaterial. Also, choice A reduces to MT/(T+M)

READING COMPREHENSION
UNDERSTANDING AND INTERPRETING WRITTEN MATERIAL
EXAMINATION SECTION
TEST 1

DIRECTIONS: Each question or incomplete statement is followed by several suggested answers or completions. Select the one that BEST answers the question or completes the statement. *PRINT THE LETTER OF THE CORRECT ANSWER IN THE SPACE AT THE RIGHT.*

Questions 1-5.

DIRECTIONS: Questions 1 through 5 are to be answered SOLELY on the basis of the following passage.

     The most effective control mechanism to prevent gross incompetence on the part of public employees is a good personnel program. The personnel officer in the line departments and the central personnel agency should exert positive leadership to raise levels of performance. Although the key factor is the quality of the personnel recruited, staff members other than personnel officers can make important contributions to efficiency. Administrative analysts, now employed in many agencies, make detailed studies of organization and procedures, with the purpose of eliminating delays, waste, and other inefficiencies. Efficiency is, however, more than a question of good organization and procedures; it is also the product of the attitudes and value of the public employees. Personal motivation can provide the will to be efficient. The best management studies will not result in substantial improvement of the performance of those employees who feel no great urge to wok up to their abilities.

1. The above passage indicates that the KEY factor in preventing gross incompetence of public employees is the
    A. hiring of administrative analysts to assist personnel people
    B. utilization of effective management studies
    C. overlapping of responsibility
    D. quality of the employees hired

2. According to the above passage, the central personnel agency staff SHOULD
    A. work more closely with administrative analysts in the line departments than with personnel officers
    B. make a serious effort to avoid jurisdictional conflicts with personnel officers in line departments
    C. contribute to improving the quality of work of public employees
    D. engage in a comprehensive program to change the public's negative image of public employees

3. The above passage indicates that efficiency in an organization can BEST be brought about by 3._____
   A. eliminating ineffective control mechanisms
   B. instituting sound organizational procedures
   C. promoting competent personnel
   D. recruiting people with desire to do good work

4. According to the above passage, the purpose of administrative analysts in a public agency is to 4._____
   A. prevent injustice to the public employee
   B. promote the efficiency of the agency
   C. protect the interests of the public
   D. ensure the observance of procedural due process

5. The above passage implies that a considerable rise in the quality of work of public employees can be brought about by 5._____
   A. encouraging positive employee attitudes toward work
   B. controlling personnel officers who exceed their powers
   C. creating warm personal associations among public employees in an agency
   D. closing loopholes in personnel organization and procedures

Questions 6-8.

DIRECTIONS: Questions 6 through 8 are to be answered SOLELY on the basis of the following passage.

EMPLOYEE NEEDS

The greatest waste in industry and in government may be that of human resources. This waste usually derives not from employees' unwillingness or inability, but from management's ineptness to meet the maintenance and motivational needs of employees. Maintenance needs refer to such needs as providing employees with safe places to work, written work rules, job security, adequate salary, employer-sponsored social activities, and with knowledge of their role in the overall framework of the organization. However, of greatest significance to employees are the motivational needs of job growth, achievement, responsibility, and recognition.

Although employee dissatisfaction may stem from either poor maintenance or poor motivation factors, the outward manifestation of the dissatisfaction may be very much like, i.e., negativism, complaints, deterioration of performance, and so forth. The improvement in the lighting of an employee's work area or raising his level of ay won't do much good if the source of the dissatisfaction is the absence of a meaningful assignment. By the same token, if an employee is dissatisfied with what he considers inequitable pay, the introduction of additional challenge in his work may simply make matters worse.

It is relatively easy for an employee to express frustration by complaining about pay, washroom conditions, fringe benefits, and so forth; but most people cannot easily express resentment in terms of the more abstract concepts concerning job growth, responsibility, and achievement.

It would be wrong to assume that there is no interaction between maintenance and motivational needs of employee. For example, conditions of high motivation often overshadow poor maintenance conditions. If an organization is in a period of strong growth and expansion, opportunities for job growth, responsibility, recognition, and achievement are usually abundant, but the rapid growth may have outrun the upkeep of maintenance factors. In this situation, motivation may be high, but only if employees recognize the poor maintenance conditions as unavoidable and temporary. The subordination of maintenance factors cannot go on indefinitely, even with the highest motivation.

Both maintenance and motivation factors influence the behavior of all employees, but employees are not identical and, furthermore, the needs of any individual do not remain orientation toward maintenance factors and those with greater sensitivity toward motivation factors.

A highly maintenance-oriented individual, preoccupied with the factors peripheral to his job rather than the job itself, is more concerned with comfort than challenge. He does not get deeply involved with his work but does with the condition of his work area, toilet facilities, and his time for going to lunch. By contrast, a strongly motivation-oriented employee is usually relatively indifferent to his surroundings and is caught up in the pursuit of work goals.

Fortunately, there are few people who are either exclusively maintenance-oriented or purely motivation-oriented. The former would be deadwood in an organization, while the latter might trample on those around him in his pursuit to achieve his goals.

6. With respect to employee motivational and maintenance needs, the management policies of an organization which is growing rapidly will probably result
   A. more in meeting motivational needs rather than maintenance needs
   B. more in meeting maintenance needs rather than motivational needs
   C. in meeting both of these needs equally
   D. in increased effort to define the motivational and maintenance needs of its employees

7. In accordance with the above passage, which of the following CANNOT be considered as an example of an employee maintenance need for railroad clerks?
   A. Providing more relief periods
   B. Providing fair salary increases at periodic intervals
   C. Increasing job responsibilities
   D. Increasing health insurance benefits

8. Most employees in an organization may be categorized as being interested in
   A. maintenance needs only
   B. motivational needs only
   C. both motivational and maintenance needs
   D. money only, to the exclusion of all other needs

Questions 9-11.

DIRECTIONS: Questions 9 through 11 are to be answered SOLELY on the basis of the following passage.

GOOD EMPLOYEE PRACTICES

As a city employee, you will be expected to take an interest in you work and perform the duties of your job to the best of your ability and in a spirit of cooperation. Nothing shows an interest in your work more than coming to work on time, not only at the start of the day but also when returning from lunch. If it is necessary for you to keep a personal appointment at lunch hour which might cause a delay in getting back to work on time, you should explain the situation to your supervisor and get his approval to come back a little late before you leave for lunch.

You should do everything that is asked of you willingly and consider important even the small jobs that your supervisor gives you. Although these jobs may seem unimportant, if you forget to do them or if you don't do them right, trouble may develop later.

Getting along well with your fellow workers will add much to the enjoyment of your work. You should respect your fellow workers and try to see their side when a disagreement arises. The better you get along with your fellow workers and your supervisor, the better you will like your job and the better you will be able to do it.

9. According to the above passage, in your job as a city employee, you are expected to
   A. show a willingness to cooperate on the job
   B. get your supervisor's approval before keeping any personal appointments at lunch hour
   C. avoid doing small jobs that seem unimportant
   D. do the easier jobs at the start of the day and the more difficult ones later on

9.____

10. According to the above passage, getting to work on time shows that you
    A. need the job
    B. have an interest in your work
    C. get along well with your fellow workers
    D. like your supervisor

10.____

11. According to the above passage, the one of the following statements that is NOT true is:
    A. If you do a small job wrong, trouble may develop
    B. You should respect your fellow workers
    C. If you disagree with a fellow worker, you should try to see his side of the story
    D. The less you get along with your supervisor, the better you will be able to do your job

11.____

Questions 12-15.

DIRECTIONS: Questions 12 through 15 are to be answered SOLELY on the basis of the following passage.

EMPLOYEE SUGGESTIONS

To increase the effectiveness of the city government, the city asks its employees to offer suggestions when they feel an improvement could be made in some government operation. The Employees' Suggestions Program was started to encourage city employees to do this. Through this Program, which is only for city employees, cash awards may be given to those whose suggestions are submitted and approved. Suggestions are looked for not only from supervisors but from all city employees as any city employee may get an idea which might be approved and contribute greatly to the solution of some problem of city government.

Therefore, all suggestions for improvement are welcome, whether they be suggestions on how to improve working conditions, or on how to increase the speed with which work is done, or on how to reduce or eliminate such things as waste, time losses, accidents or fire hazards. There are, however, a few types of suggestions for which cash awards cannot be given. An example of this type would be a suggestion to increase salaries or a suggestion to change the regulations about annual leave or about sick leave. The number of suggestions sent in has increased sharply during the past few years. It is hoped that it will keep increasing in the future in order to meet the city's needs for more ideas for improved ways of doing things.

12. According to the above passage, the MAIN reason why the city asks its employees for suggestions about government operations is to
    A. increase the effectiveness of the city government
    B. show that the Employees' Suggestion Program is working well
    C. show that everybody helps run the city government
    D. have the employee win a prize

13. According to the above passage, the Employees' Suggestion Program can approve awards ONLY for those suggestions that come from
    A. city employees
    B. city employees who are supervisors
    C. city employees who are not supervisors
    D. experienced employee of the city

14. According to the above passage, a cash award cannot be given through the Employees' Suggestion Program for a suggestion about
    A. getting work done faster
    B. helping prevent accidents on the job
    C. increasing the amount of annual leave for city employees
    D. reducing the chance of fire where city employees work

15. According to the above passage, the suggestions sent in during the past few years have 15.____
    A. all been approved
    B. generally been well written
    C. been mostly about reducing or eliminating waste
    D. been greater in number than before

Questions 16-18.

DIRECTIONS: Questions 16 through 18 are to be answered SOLELY on the basis of the following passage.

    The supervisor will gain the respect of the members of his staff and increase his influence over them by controlling his temper and avoiding criticizing anyone publicly. When a mistake is made, the good supervisor will take it over with the employee quietly and privately. The supervisor will listen to the employee's story, suggest the better way of doing the job, and offer help so the mistake won't happen again. Before closing the discussion, the supervisor should try to find something good to say about other parts of the employee's work. Some praise and appreciation, along with instruction, is more likely to encourage an employee to improve in those areas where he is weakest.

16. A good title that would show the meaning of the above passage would be 16.____
    A. How to Correct Employee Errors
    B. How to Praise Employees
    C. Mistakes are Preventable
    D. The Weak Employee

17. According to the above passage, the work of an employee who has made a mistake is more likely to improve if the supervisor 17.____
    A. avoids criticizing him
    B. gives him a chance to suggest a better way of doing the work
    C. listens to the employee's excuses to see if he is right
    D. praises good work at the same time he corrects the mistake

18. According to the above passage, when a supervisor needs to correct an employee's mistake, it is important that he 18.____
    A. allow some time to go by after the mistake is made
    B. do so when other employee are not present
    C. show his influence with his tone of voice
    D. tell other employee to avoid the same mistake

Questions 19-23.

DIRECTIONS: Questions 19 through 23 are to be answered SOLELY on the basis of the following passage.

    In studying the relationships of people to the organizational structure, it is absolutely necessary to identify and recognize the informal organizational structure. These relationships are necessary when coordination of a plan is attempted. They may be with *the boss*, line supervisors, staff personnel, or other representatives of the formal organization's hierarchy, and they may include the *liaison men* who serve as the leaders of the informal organization. An acquaintanceship with the people serving in these roles in the organization, and its formal counterpart, permits a supervisor to recognize sensitive areas in which it is simple to get conflict reaction. Avoidance of such areas, plus conscious efforts to inform other people of his own objectives for various plans, will usually enlist their aid and support. Planning *without* people can lead to disaster because the individuals who must act together to make any plan a success are more important than the plans themselves.

19. Of the following titles, the one that MOST clearly describes the above passage is
    A. Coordination of a Function
    B. Avoidance of Conflict
    C. Planning With People
    D. Planning Objectives

20. According to the above passage, attempts at coordinating plans may fail unless
    A. the plan's objectives are clearly set forth
    B. conflict between groups is resolved
    C. the plans themselves are worthwhile
    D. informal relationships are recognized

21. According to the above passage, conflict
    A. may, in some cases, be desirable to secure results
    B. produces more heat than light
    C. should be avoided at all costs
    D. possibilities can be predicted by a sensitive supervisor

22. The above passage implies that
    A. informal relationships are more important than formal structure
    B. the weakness of a formal structure depends upon informal relationships
    C. liaison men are the key people to consult when taking formal and informal structures into account
    D. individuals in a group are at least as important as the plans for the group

23. The above passage suggests that
    A. some planning can be disastrous
    B. certain people in sensitive areas should be avoided
    C. the supervisor should discourage acquaintanceships in the organization
    D. organizational relationships should be consciously limited

Questions 24-25.

DIRECTIONS: Questions 24 and 25 are to be answered SOLELY on the basis of the following passage.

Good personnel relations of an organization depend upon mutual confidence, trust, and good will. The basis of confidence is understanding. Most troubles start with people who do not understand each other. When the organization's intentions or motives are misunderstood, or when reasons for actions, practices, or policies are misconstrued, complete cooperation from individuals is not forthcoming. If management expects full cooperation from employees, it has a responsibility of sharing with them the information which is the foundation of proper understanding, confidence, and trust. Personnel management has long since outgrown the days when it was the vogue to *treat them rough and tell them nothing*. Up-to-date personnel management provides all possible information about the activities, aims, and purposes of the organization. It seems altogether creditable that a desire should exist among employees for such information which the best-intentioned executive might think would not interest them and which the worst-intentioned would think was none of their business.

24. The above passage implies that one of the causes of the difficulty which an organization might have with its personnel relations is that its employees
    A. have not expressed interest in the activities, aims, and purposes of the organization
    B. do not believe in the good faith of the organization
    C. have not been able to give full cooperation to the organization
    D. do not recommend improvements in the practices and policies of the organization

25. According to the above passage, in order for an organization to have good personnel relations, it is NOT essential that
    A. employees have confidence in the organization
    B. the purposes of the organization be understood by the employees
    C. employees have a desire for information about the organization
    D. information about the organization be communicated to employees

KEY (CORRECT ANSWERS)

1.	D		11.	D
2.	C		12.	A
3.	D		13.	A
4.	B		14.	C
5.	A		15.	D
6.	A		16.	A
7.	C		17.	D
8.	C		18.	B
9.	A		19.	C
10.	B		20.	D

21.	D
22.	D
23.	A
24.	B
25.	C

TEST 2

DIRECTIONS: Each question or incomplete statement is followed by several suggested answers or completions. Select the one that BEST answers the question or completes the statement. *PRINT THE LETTER OF THE CORRECT ANSWER IN THE SPACE AT THE RIGHT.*

Questions 1-8.

DIRECTIONS: Questions 1 through 8 are to be answered SOLELY on the basis of the following passage.

    Important figures in education and in public affairs have recommended development of a private organization sponsored in part by various private foundations which would offer installment payment plans to full-time matriculated students in accredited colleges and universities in the United States and Canada. Contracts would be drawn to cover either tuition and fees, or tuition, fees, room and board in college facilities, from one year up to and including six years. A special charge, which would vary with the length of the contract, would be added to the gross repayable amount. This would be in addition to interest at a rate which would vary with the income of the parents. There would be a 3% annual interest charge for families with total income, before income taxes, of $50,000 or less. The rate would increase by 1/10 of 1% for every $1,000 of additional net income in excess of $50,000 up to a maximum of 10% interest. Contracts would carry an insurance provision on the life of the parent or guardian who signs the contract; all contracts must have the signature of a parent or guardian. Payment would be scheduled in equal monthly installments.

1. Which of the following students would be eligible for the payment plan described in the above passage? A
   A. matriculated student taking six semester hours toward a graduate degree
   B. matriculated student taking seventeen semester hours toward an undergraduate degree
   C. graduate matriculated at the University of Mexico taking eighteen semester hours toward a graduate degree
   D. student taking eighteen semester hours in a special pre-matriculation program

    1.____

2. According to the above passage, the organization described would be sponsored in part by
   A. private foundations   B. colleges and universities
   C. persons in the field of education   D. persons in public life

    2.____

3. Which of the following expenses could NOT be covered by a contract with the organization described in the above passage?
   A. Tuition amounting to $20,000 per year
   B. Registration and laboratory fees
   C. Meals at restaurants near the college
   D. Rent for an apartment in a college dormitory

    3.____

165

4. The total amount to be paid would include ONLY the
   A. principal
   B. principal and interest
   C. principal, interest, and special charge
   D. principal, interest, special charge, and fee

5. The contract would carry insurance on the
   A. life of the student
   B. life of the student's parents
   C. income of the parents of the student
   D. life of the parent who signed the contract

6. The interest rate for an annual loan of $25,000 from the organization described in the above passage for a student whose family's net income was $55,000 should be
   A. 3%   B. 3.5%   C. 4%   D. 4.5%

7. The interest rate for an annual loan of $35,000 from the organization described in the above passage for a student whose family's net income was $100,000 should be
   A. 5%   B. 8%   C. 9%   D. 10%

8. John Lee has submitted an application for the installment payment plan described in the above passage. John's mother and father have a store which grossed $500,000 last year, but the income which the family received from the store was $90,000 before taxes. They also had $5,000 income from stock dividends. They paid $10,000 in income taxes.
   The amount of income upon which the interest should be based is
   A. $85,000   B. $90,000   C. $95,000   D. $105,000

Questions 9-13.

DIRECTIONS: Questions 9 through 13 are to be answered SOLELY on the basis of the following passage.

Since the organization chart is pictorial in nature, there is a tendency for it to be drawn in an artistically balanced and appealing fashion, regardless of the realities of actual organizational structure. In addition to being subject to this distortion, there is the difficulty of communicating in any organization chart the relative importance or the relative size of various component parts of an organizational structure. Furthermore, because of the need for simplicity of design, an organization chart can never indicate the full extent of the interrelationships among the component parts of an organization.

These interrelationships are often just as vital as the specifications which an organization chart endeavors to indicate. Yet, if an organization chart were to be drawn with all the wide variety of criss-crossing communication and cooperation networks existent within a typical organization, the chart would probably be much more confusing than informative. It is also obvious that no organization chart as such can prove or disprove that the organizational structure it represents is effective in realizing the objectives of the organization. At best, an organization chart can only illustrate some of the various factors to be taken into consideration in understanding, devising, or altering organizational arrangements.

9. According to the above passage, an organization chart can be expected to portray the
   A. structure of the organization along somewhat ideal lines
   B. relative size of the organizational units quite accurately
   C. channels of information distribution within the organization graphically
   D. extent of the obligation of each unit to meet the organizational objectives

10. According to the above passage, those aspects of internal functioning which are NOT shown on an organization chart
    A. can be considered to have little practical application in the operations of the organization
    B. might well be considered to be as important as the structural relationships which a chart does present
    C. could be the cause of considerable confusion in the operations of an organization which is quite large
    D. would be most likely to provide the information needed to determine the overall effectiveness of an organization

11. In the above passage, the one of the following conditions which is NOT implied as being a defect of an organization chart is that an organization chart may
    A. present a picture of the organizational structure which is different from the structure that actually exists
    B. fail to indicate the comparative size of various organizational units
    C. be limited in its ability to convey some of the meaningful aspects of organizational relationships
    D. become less useful over a period of time during which the organizational facts which it illustrated have changed

12. The one of the following which is the MOST suitable title for the above passage is
    A. The Design and Construction of an Organization Chart
    B. The Informal Aspects of an Organization Chart
    C. The Inherent Deficiencies of an Organization Chart
    D. The Utilization of a Typical Organization Chart

13. It can be inferred from the above passage that the function of an organization chart is to
    A. contribute to the comprehension of the organization form and arrangements
    B. establish the capabilities of the organization to operate effectively
    C. provide a balanced picture of the operations of the organization
    D. eliminate the need for complexity in the organization's structure

Questions 14-16.

DIRECTIONS: Questions 14 through 16 are to be answered SOLELY on the basis of the following passage.

In dealing with visitors to the school office, the school secretary must use initiative, tact, and good judgment. All visitors should be greeted promptly and courteously. The nature of their business should be determined quickly and handled expeditiously. Frequently, the secretary should be able to handle requests, deliveries, or passes herself. Her judgment should determine when a visitor should see members of the staff or the principal. Serious problems or doubtful cases should be referred to a supervisor.

14. In general, visitors should be handled by the 14.____
    A. school secretary
    B. principal
    C. appropriate supervisor
    D. person who is free

15. It is wise to obtain the following information from visitors: 15.____
    A. Name
    B. Nature of business
    C. Address
    D. Problems they have

16. All visitors who wish to see members of the staff should 16.____
    A. be permitted to do so
    B. produce identification
    C. do so for valid reasons only
    D. be processed by a supervisor

Questions 17-19.

DIRECTIONS: Questions 17 through 19 are to be answered SOLELY on the basis of the following passage.

Information regarding payroll status, salary differentials, promotional salary increments, deductions, and pension payments should be given to all members of the staff who have questions regarding these items. On occasion, if the secretary is uncertain regarding the information, the staff member should be referred to the principal or the appropriate agency. No question by a staff member regarding payroll status should be brushed aside as immaterial or irrelevant. The school secretary must always try to handle the question or pass it on to the person who can handle it.

17. If a teacher is dissatisfied with information regarding her salary status, as given 17.____
    by the school secretary, the matter should be
    A. dropped
    B. passed on to the principal
    C. passed on by the secretary to proper agency or the principal
    D. made a basis for grievance procedures

18. The following is an adequate summary of the above passage: 18.____
    A. The secretary must handle all payroll matters
    B. The secretary must handle all payroll matter or know who can handle them
    C. The secretary or the principal must handle all payroll matters
    D. Payroll matter too difficult to handle must be followed up until they are solved

19. The above passage implies that 19.____
    A. many teachers ask immaterial questions regarding payroll status
    B. few teachers ask irrelevant pension questions
    C. no teachers ask immaterial salary questions
    D. no question regarding salary should be considered irrelevant

Questions 20-22.

DIRECTIONS: Questions 20 through 22 are to be answered SOLELY on the basis of the following passage.

The necessity for good speech on the part of the school secretary cannot be overstated. The school secretary must deal with the general public, the pupils, the members of the staff, and the school supervisors. In every situation which involves the general public, the secretary serves as a representative of the school. In dealing with pupils, the secretary's speech must serve as a model from which students may guide themselves. Slang, colloquialisms, malapropisms, and local dialects must be avoided.

20. The above passage implies that the speech pattern of the secretary must be 20.____
    A. perfect
    B. very good
    C. average
    D. on a level with that of the pupils

21. The last sentence indicates that slang 21.____
    A. is acceptable
    B. occurs in all speech
    C. might be used occasionally
    D. should be shunned

22. The above passage implies that the speech of pupils 22.____
    A. may be influenced
    B. does not change readily
    C. is generally good
    D. is generally poor

Questions 23-25.

DIRECTIONS: Questions 23 through 25 are to be answered SOLELY on the basis of the following passage.

The school secretary who is engaged in the task of filing records and correspondence should follow a general set of rules. Items which are filed should be available to other secretaries or to supervisors quickly and easily by means of the application of a modicum of common sense and good judgment. Items which, by their nature, may be difficult to find should be cross-indexed. Folders and drawers should be neatly and accurately labeled. There should never be a large accumulation of papers which have not been filed.

23. A good general rule to follow in filing is that materials should be 23.____
    A. placed in folders quickly
    B. neatly stored
    C. readily available
    D. cross-indexed

24. Items that are filed should be available to
    A. the secretary charged with the task of filing
    B. secretaries and supervisors
    C. school personnel
    D. the principal

    24.____

25. A modicum of common sense means _____ common sense.
    A. an average amount of   B. a great deal of
    C. a little   D. no

    25.____

KEY (CORRECT ANSWERS)

1.	B		11.	D
2.	A		12.	C
3.	C		13.	A
4.	C		14.	A
5.	D		15.	B
6.	B		16.	C
7.	B		17.	C
8.	C		18.	B
9.	A		19.	D
10.	B		20.	B

21. D
22. A
23. C
24. B
25. C

TEST 3

DIRECTIONS: Each question or incomplete statement is followed by several suggested answers or completions. Select the one that BEST answers the question or completes the statement. *PRINT THE LETTER OF THE CORRECT ANSWER IN THE SPACE AT THE RIGHT.*

Questions 1-4.

DIRECTIONS: Questions 1 through 4 are to be answered SOLELY on the basis of the following passage.

The proposition that administrative activity is essentially the same in all organizations appears to underlie some of the practices in the administration of private higher education. Although the practice is unusual in public education, there are numerous instances of industrial, governmental, or military administrators being assigned to private institutions of higher education and, to a lesser extent, of college and university presidents assuming administrative positions in other types of organizations. To test this theory that administrators are interchangeable, there is a need for systematic observation and classification. The myth that an educational administrator must first have experience in the teaching profession is firmly rooted in a long tradition that has historical prestige. The myth is bound up in the expectations of the public and personnel surrounding the administrator. Since administrative success depends significantly on how well an administrator meets the expectations others have of him, the myth may be more powerful than the special experience in helping the administrator attain organizational and educational objectives. Educational administrators who have risen through the teaching profession have often expressed nostalgia for the life of a teacher or scholar, but there is no evidence that this nostalgia contributes to administrative success.

1. Which of the following statements as completed is MOST consistent with the above passage?
   The greatest number of administrators has moved from
   A. industry and the military to government and universities
   B. government and universities to industry and the military
   C. government, the armed forces, and industry to colleges and universities
   D. colleges and universities to government, the armed forces, and industry

1.____

2. Of the following, the MOST reasonable inference from the above passage is that a specific area requiring further research is the
   A. place of myth in the tradition and history of the educational profession
   B. relative effectiveness of educational administrators from inside and outside the teaching profession
   C. performance of administrators in the administration of public colleges
   D. degree of reality behind the nostalgia for scholarly pursuits often expressed by educational administrators

2.____

3. According to the above passage, the value to an educational administrator of experience in the teaching profession
   A. lies in the first-hand knowledge he has acquired of immediate educational problems
   B. may lie in the belief of his colleagues, subordinates, and the public that such experience is necessary
   C. has been supported by evidence that the experience contributes to administrative success in educational fields
   D. would be greater if the administrator were able to free himself from nostalgia for his former duties

3._____

4. Of the following, the MOST suitable title for the above passage is
   A. Educational Administration, Its Problems
   B. The Experience Needed For Educational Administration
   C. Administration in Higher Education
   D. Evaluating Administrative Experience

4._____

Questions 5-6.

DIRECTIONS: Questions 5 and 6 are to be answered SOLELY on the basis of the following passage.

Management by objectives (MBO) may be defined as the process by which the superior and the subordinate managers of an organization jointly define its common goals, define each individual's major areas of responsibility in terms of the results expected of him and use these measure as guides for operating the unit and assessing the contribution of each of its members.

The MBO approach requires that after organizational goals are established and communicated, targets must be set for each individual position which are congruent with organizational goals. Periodic performance reviews and a final review using the objectives set as criteria are also basic to this approach.

Recent studies have shown that MBO programs are influenced by attitudes and perceptions of the boss, the company, the reward-punishment system, and the program itself. In addition, the manner in which the MBO program is carried out can influence the success of the program. A study done in the late sixties indicates that the best results are obtained when the manager sets goals which deal with significant problem areas in the organizational unit, or with the subordinate's personal deficiencies. These goals must be clear with regard to what is expected of the subordinate. The frequency of feedback is also important in the success of a management-by-objectives program. Generally, the greater the amount of feedback, the more successful the MBO program.

5. According to the above passage, the expected output for individual employees should be determined
   A. after a number of reviews of work performance
   B. after common organizational goals are defined
   C. before common organizational goals are defined
   D. on the basis of an employee's personal qualities

5._____

6. According to the above passage, the management-by-objectives approach requires
   A. less feedback than other types of management programs
   B. little review of on-the-job performance after the initial setting of goals
   C. general conformance between individual goals and organizational goals
   D. the setting of goals which deal with minor problem areas in the organization

Questions 7-10.

DIRECTIONS: Questions 7 through 10 are to be answered SOLELY on the basis of the following passage.

Management, which is the function of executive leadership, has as its principal phases the planning, organizing, and controlling of the activities of subordinate groups in the accomplishment of organizational objectives. Planning specifies the kind and extent of the factors, forces, and effects, and the relationships among them, that will be required for satisfactory accomplishment. The nature of the objectives and their requirements must be known before determinations can be made as to what must be done, how it must be done and why, where actions should take place, who should be responsible, and similar programs pertaining to the formulation of a plan. Organizing, which creates the conditions that must be present before the execution of the plan can be undertaken successfully, cannot be done intelligently without knowledge of the organizational objectives. Control, which has to do with the constraint and regulation of activities entering into the execution of the plan, must be exercised in accordance with the characteristics and requirements of the activities demanded by the plan.

7. The one of the following which is the MOST suitable title for the above passage is
   A. The Nature of Successful Organization
   B. The Planning of Management Functions
   C. The Importance of Organizational Functions
   D. The Principle Aspects of Management

8. It can be inferred from the above passage that the one of the following functions whose existence is essential to the existence of the other three is the
   A. regulation of the work needed to carry out a plan
   B. understanding of what the organization intends to accomplish
   C. securing of information of the factors necessary for accomplishment of objectives
   D. establishment of the conditions required for successful action

9. The one of the following which would NOT be included within any of the principal phases of the function of executive leadership as defined in the above passage is
   A. determination of manpower requirements
   B. procurement of required material
   C. establishment of organizational objectives
   D. scheduling of production

10. The conclusion which can MOST reasonably be drawn from the above passage   10.____
    is that the control phase of managing is most directly concerned with the
    A. influencing of policy determinations
    B. administering of suggestion systems
    C. acquisition of staff for the organization
    D. implementation of performance standards

Questions 11-12.

DIRECTIONS: Questions 11 and 12 are to be answered SOLELY on the basis of the following passage.

Under an open-and-above-board policy, it is to be expected that some supervisors will gloss over known shortcomings of subordinates rather than face the task of discussing team face-to-face. It is also to be expected that at least some employees whose job performance is below par will reject the supervisor's appraisal as biased and unfair. Be that as it may, these are inescapable aspects of any performance appraisal system in which human beings are involved. The supervisor who shies away from calling a spade a spade, as well as the employee with a chip on his shoulder, will each in his own way eventually be revealed in his true light—to the benefit of the organization as a whole.

11. The BEST of the following interpretations of the above passage is that   11.____
    A. the method of rating employee performance requires immediate revision to improve employee acceptance
    B. substandard performance ratings should be discussed with employees even if satisfactory ratings are not
    C. supervisors run the risk of being called unfair by the subordinates even though their appraisals are accurate
    D. any system of employee performance rating is satisfactory if used properly

12. The BEST of the following interpretations of the above passage is that   12.____
    A. supervisors generally are not open-and-above-board with their subordinates
    B. it is necessary for supervisors to tell employees objectively how they are performing
    C. employees complain when their supervisor does not keep them informed
    D. supervisors are afraid to tell subordinates their weaknesses

Questions 13-15.

DIRECTIONS: Questions 13 through 15 are to be answered SOLELY on the basis of the following passage.

During the last decade, a great deal of interest has been generated around the phenomenon of *organizational development,* or the process of developing human resources through conscious organization effort. Organizational development (OD) stresses improving interpersonal relationships and organizational skills, such as communication, to a much greater degree than individual training ever did. The kind of training that an organization should emphasize depends upon the present and future structure of the organization. If future organizations are to be unstable, shifting coalitions, then individual skills and abilities, particularly those emphasizing innovativeness, creativity, flexibility, and the latest technological knowledge, are crucial and individual training is most appropriate.

But if there is to be little change in organizational structure, then the main thrust of training should be group-oriented or organizational development. This approach seems better designed for overcoming hierarchical barriers, for developing a degree of interpersonal relationships which make communication along the chain of command possible, and for retaining a modicum of innovation and/or flexibility.

13. According to the above passage, group-oriented training is MOST useful in in
   A. developing a communications system that will facilitate understanding through the chain of command
   B. highly flexible and mobile organizations
   C. preventing the crossing of hierarchical barriers within an organization
   D. saving energy otherwise wasted on developing methods of dealing with rigid hierarchies

14. The one of the following conclusions which can be drawn MOST appropriately from the above passage is that
   A. behavioral research supports the use of organizational development training methods rather than individualized training
   B. it is easier to provide individualized training in specific skills than to set up sensitivity training programs
   C. organizational development eliminates innovative or flexible activity
   D. the nature of an organization greatly influences which training methods will be most effective

15. According to the above passage, the one of the following which is LEAST important for large-scale organizations geared to rapid and abrupt change is
   A. current technological information
   B. development of a high degree of interpersonal relationships
   C. development of individual skills and abilities
   D. emphasis on creativity

Questions 16-18.

DIRECTIONS: Questions 16 through 18 are to be answered SOLELY on the basis of the following passage.

The increase in the extent to which each individual is personally responsible to others is most noticeable in a large bureaucracy. No one person *decides* anything; each decision of any importance, is the product of an intricate process of brokerage involving individuals inside and outside the organization who feel some reason to be affected by the decision, or two have special knowledge to contribute to it. The more varied the organization's constituency, the more inside *veto-groups* will need to be taken into account. But even if no outside consultations were involved, sheer size would produce a complex process of decision. For a large organization is a deliberately created system of tensions into which each individual is expected to bring work-ways, viewpoints, and outside relationships markedly different from those of his colleagues. It is the administrator's task to draw from these disparate forces the elements of wise action from day to day, consistent with the purposes of the organization as a whole.

16. The above passage is essentially a description of decision-making as 16._____
    A. an organization process
    B. the key responsibility of the administrator
    C. the one best position among many
    D. a complex of individual decisions

17. Which one of the following statements BEST describes the responsibilities of 17._____
    an administrator?
    A. He modifies decisions and goals in accordance with pressures from within and outside the organization.
    B. He creates problem-solving mechanisms that rely on the varied interests of his staff and *veto-groups*.
    C. He makes determinations that will lead to attainment of his agency's objectives.
    D. He obtains agreement among varying viewpoints and interests

18. In the context of the operations of a central public personnel agency, a 18._____
    veto-group would LEAST likely consist of
    A. employee organizations
    B. professional personnel societies
    C. using agencies
    D. civil service newspapers

Questions 19-25.

DIRECTIONS: Questions 19 through 25 are to be answered SOLELY on the basis of the following passage, which is an extract from a report prepared for Department X, which outlines the procedure to be followed in the case of transfers of employees.

Every transfer, regardless of the reason therefore, requires completion of the record of transfer, Form DT411. To denote consent to the transfer, DT411 should contain the signatures of the transferee and the personnel officer(s) concerned, except that, in the case of an involuntary transfer, the signatures of the transferee's present and prospective supervisors shall be entered in Boxes 8A and 8B, respectively, since the transferee does not consent. Only a permanent employee may request a transfer; in such cases, the employee's attendance record shall be duly considered with regard to absences, latenesses, and accrued overtime balances. In the case of an inter-district transfer, the employee's attendance record must be included in Section 8A of the transfer request, Form DT410, by the personnel officer of the district from which the transfer is requested. The personnel officer of the district to which the employee requested transfer may refuse to accept accrued overtime balances in excess of ten days.

An employee on probation shall be eligible for transfer. If such employee is involuntarily transferred, he shall be credited for the period of time already served on probation. However, if such transfer is voluntary, the employee shall be required to serve the entire period of his probation in the new position. An employee who has occurred a disability which prevents him from performing his normal duties may be transferred during the period of such disability to other appropriate duties. A disability transfer requires the completion of either DT414 if the disability is job-connected, or Form DT415 if it is not a job-connected disability. In either case, the personnel officer of the district from which the transfer is made signs in Box 6A of the first two copies and the personnel officer of the district to which the transfer is made signs in Box 6B of the last two copies, or, in the case of an intra-district disability transfer, the personnel officer must sign in Box 6A of the first two copies and Box 6B of the last two copies.

19. When a personnel officer consents to an employee's request for transfer from his district, this procedure requires that the personnel officer sign Forms
    A. DT411
    B. DT410 and DT411
    C. DT411 and either Form DT414 or DT415
    D. DT410 and DT411, and either Form DT414 or DT415

20. With respect to the time record of an employee transferred against his wishes during his probationary period, this procedure requires that
    A. he serve the entire period of his probation in his present office
    B. he lose his accrued overtime balance
    C. his attendance record be considered with regard to absences and latenesses
    D. he be given credit for the period of time he has already served on probation

21. Assume you are a supervisor and an employee must be transferred into your office against his wishes.
    According to this procedure, the box you must sign on the record of transfer is
    A. 6A   B. 8A   C. 6B   D. 8B

22. Under this procedure, in the case of a disability transfer, when must Box 6A on Forms DT414 and DT415 be signed by the personnel officer of the district to which the transfer is being made?
    A. In all cases when either Form DT414 or Form DT415 is used
    B. In all cases when Form DT414 is used and only under certain circumstances when Form DT415 is used
    C. In all cases when Form DT415 is used and only under certain circumstances when Form DT414 is used
    D. Only under certain circumstances when either Form DT414 or Form DT415 is used

8 (#3)

23. From the above passage, it may be inferred MOST correctly that the number of copies of Form DT414 is
    A. no more than 2
    B. at least 3
    C. at least 5
    D. more than the number of copies of Form DT415

24. A change in punctuation and capitalization only which would change one sentence into two and possibly contribute to somewhat greater ease of reading this report extract would be MOST appropriate in the
    A. 2nd sentence, 1st paragraph
    B. 3rd sentence, 1st paragraph
    C. next to the last sentence, 2nd paragraph
    D. 2nd sentence, 2nd paragraph

25. In the second paragraph, a word that is INCORRECTLY used is
    A. *shall* in the 1st sentence
    B. *voluntary* in the 3rd sentence
    C. *occurred* in the 4th sentence
    D. *intra-district* in the last sentence

KEY (CORRECT ANSWERS)

1.	C		11.	C
2.	B		12.	B
3.	B		13.	A
4.	B		14.	D
5.	B		15.	B
6.	C		16.	A
7.	D		17.	C
8.	B		18.	B
9.	C		19.	A
10.	D		20.	D

21.	D
22.	D
23.	B
24.	B
25.	C

PREPARING WRITTEN MATERIALS
EXAMINATION SECTION
TEST 1

DIRECTIONS: Each question or incomplete statement is followed by several suggested answers or completions. Select the one that BEST answers the question or completes the statement. *PRINT THE LETTER OF THE CORRECT ANSWER IN THE SPACE AT THE RIGHT.*

Questions 1-21.

DIRECTIONS: In each of the following sentences, which were taken from students' transcripts, there may be an error. Indicate the appropriate correction in the space at the right. If the sentence is correct as is, indicate this choice. Unnecessary changes will be considered incorrect.

1. In that building there seemed to be representatives of Teachers College, the Veterans Bureau, and the Businessmen's Association.
   A. Teacher's College
   B. Veterans' Bureau
   C. Businessmens Association
   D. Correct as is

   1.____

2. In his travels, he visited St. Paul, San Francisco, Springfield, Ohio, and Washington, D.C.
   A. Ohio and
   B. Saint Paul
   C. Washington, D.C.
   D. Correct as is

   2.____

3. As a result of their purchasing a controlling interest in the syndicate, it was well-known that the Bureau of Labor Statistics' calculations would be unimportant.
   A. of them purchasing
   B. well known
   C. Statistics
   D. Correct as is

   3.____

4. Walter Scott, Jr.'s, attempt to emulate his father's success was doomed to failure.
   A. Junior's,
   B. Scott's, Jr.
   C. Scott, Jr.'s attempt
   D. Correct as is

   4.____

5. About B.C. 250 the Romans invaded Great Britain, and remains of their highly developed civilization can still be seen.
   A. 250 B.C.
   Britain and
   C. highly-developed
   D. Correct as is

   5.____

6. The two boss's sons visited the children's department.
   A. bosses
   B. bosses'
   C. childrens'
   D. Correct as is

   6.____

7. Miss Amex not only approved the report, but also decided that it needed no revision.
   A. report; but   B. report but   C. report. But   D. Correct as is

8. Here's brain food in a jiffy—economical, too!
   A. economical too!
   B. "brain food"
   C. jiffy-economical
   D. Correct as is

9. She said, "He likes the "Gatsby Look" very much."
   A. said "He
   B. "he
   C. 'Gatsby Look'
   D. Correct as is

10. We anticipate that we will be able to visit them briefly in Los Angeles on Wednesday after a five day visit.
    A. Wednes-   B. 5 day   C. five-day   D. Correct as is

11. She passed all her tests, and, she now has a good position.
    A. tests, and she
    B. past
    C. tests;
    D. Correct as is

12. The billing clerk said, "I will send the bill today"; however, that was a week ago, and it hasn't arrived yet!
    A. today;"   B. today,"   C. ago and   D. Correct as is

13. "She types at more-than-average speed," Miss Smith said, "but I feel that it is a result of marvelous concentration and self control on her part."
    A. more than average
    B. "But
    C. self-control
    D. Correct as is

14. The state of Alaska, the largest state in the union, is also the northernmost state.
    A. Union
    B. Northernmost State
    C. State of Alaska
    D. Correct as is

15. The memoirs of Ex-President Nixon, according to figures, sold more copies than Six Crises, the book he wrote in the '60s.
    A. Six Crises
    B. ex-President
    C. 60s
    D. Correct as is

16. "There are three principal elements, determining the hazard of buildings: the contents hazard, the fire resistance of the structure, and the character of the interior finish," concluded the speaker.
    The one of the following statements that is MOST acceptable is that, in the above passage,
    A. the comma following the word *elements* is incorrect
    B. the colon following the word *buildings* is incorrect
    C. the comma following the word *finish* is incorrect
    D. there is no error in the punctuation of the sentence

17. He spoke on his favorite topic, "Why We Will Win." (How could I stop him?) 17._____
    A. Win". B. him?). C. him)? C. Correct as is

18. "All any insurance policy is, is a contract for services," said my insurance 18._____
    agent, Mr. Newton.
    A. Insurance Policy   B. Insurance Agent
    C. policy is is a   D. Correct as is

19. Inasmuch as the price list has now been up dated, we should sent it to the 19._____
    printer.
    A. In as much   B. updated
    C. pricelist   D. Correct as is

20. We feel that "Our know-how" is responsible for the improvement in technical 20._____
    developments.
    A. "our   B. know how   C. that,   D. Correct as is

21. Did Cortez conquer the Incas? the Aztecs? the South American Indians? 21._____
    A. Incas, the Aztecs, the South American Indians?
    B. Incas; the Aztecs; the South American Indians?
    C. south American Indians?
    D. Correct as is

22. Which one of the following forms for the typed name of the dictator in the closing 22._____
    lines of a letter is generally MOST acceptable in the United States?
    A. (Dr.) James F. Farley   B. Dr. James F. Farley
    C. Me. James J. Farley, Ph.D.   D. James F. Farley

23. The plural of 23._____
    A. turkey is turkies   B. cargo is cargoes
    C. bankruptcy is bankruptcys   D. son-in-law is son-in-laws

24. The abbreviation viz. means MOST NEARLY 24._____
    A. namely   B. for example
    C. the following   D. see

25. In the sentence, *A man in a light-gray suit waited thirty-five minutes in the* 25._____
    ante-room for the all-important document, the word IMPROPERLY hyphenated
    is
    A. light-gray   B. thirty-five   C. ante-room   D. all-important

KEY (CORRECT ANSWERS)

1. D
2. C
3. B
4. D
5. A

6. B
7. B
8. D
9. C
10. C

11. A
12. D
13. D
14. A
15. B

16. A
17. D
18. D
19. B
20. A

21. D
22. D
23. B
24. A
25. C

TEST 2

DIRECTIONS: Each question or incomplete statement is followed by several suggested answers or completions. Select the one that BEST answers the question or completes the statement. *PRINT THE LETTER OF THE CORRECT ANSWER IN THE SPACE AT THE RIGHT.*

Questions 1-10.

DIRECTIONS: In each of the following groups of four sentences, one sentence contains an error in sentence structure, grammar, usage, diction, or punctuation. Indicate the INCORRECT sentence.

1. A. The lecture finished, the audience began asking questions.
   B. Any man who could accomplish that task the world would regard as a hero.
   C. Our respect and admiration are mutual.
   D. George did like his mother told him, despite the importunities of his playmates.

2. A. I cannot but help admiring you for your dedication to your job.
   B. Because they had insisted upon showing us films of their travels, we have lost many friends whom we once cherished.
   C. I am constrained to admit that your remarks made me feel bad.
   D. My brother having been notified of his acceptance by the university of his choice, my father immediately made plans for a vacation.

3. A. In no other country is freedom of speech and assembly so jealously guarded.
   B. Being a beatnik, he felt that it would be a betrayal of his cause to wear shoes and socks at the same time.
   C. Riding over the Brooklyn Bridge gave us an opportunity to see the Manhattan skyline.
   D. In 1961, flaunting SEATO, the North Vietnamese crossed the line of demarcation.

4. A. I have enjoyed the study of the Spanish language not only because of its beauty and the opportunity it offers to understand the Hispanic culture but also to make use of it in the business associations I have in South America.
   B. The opinions he expressed were decidedly different from those he had held in his youth.
   C. Had he actually studied, he certainly would have passed.
   D. A supervisor should be patient, tactful, and firm.

5. A. At this point we were faced with only three alternatives: to push on, to remain where we were, or to return to the village.
   B. We had no choice but to forgive so venial a sin.
   C. In their new picture, the Warners are flouting tradition.
   D. Photographs taken revealed that 2.5 square miles had been burned.

6. A. He asked whether he might write to his friends.
    B. There are many problems which must be solved before we can be assured of world peace.
    C. Each person with whom I talked expressed his opinion freely.
    D. Holding on to my saddle with all my strength the horse galloped down the road at a terrifying pace.

7. A. After graduating high school, he obtained a position as a runner in Wall Street.
    B. Last night, in a radio address, the President urged us to subscribe to the Red Cross.
    C. In the evening, light spring rain cooled the streets.
    D. "Un-American" is a word which has been used even by those whose sympathies may well have been pro-Nazi.

8. A. It is hard to conceive of their not doing good work.
    B. Who won—you or I?
    C. He having read the speech caused much comment.
    D. Their finishing the work proves that it can be done.

9. A. Our course of study should not be different now than it was five years ago.
    B. I cannot deny myself the pleasure of publicly thanking the mayor for his actions.
    C. The article on "Morale" has appeared in the Times Literary Supplement.
    D. He died of tuberculosis contracted during service with the Allied Forces.

10. A. If it wasn't for a lucky accident, he would still be an office-clerk.
    B. It is evident that teachers need help.
    C. Rolls of postage stamps may be bought at stationery stores.
    D. Addressing machines are used by firms that publish magazines.

11. The one of the following sentences which contains NO error in usage is:
    A. After the robbers left, the proprietor stood tied in his chair for about two hours before help arrived.
    B. In the cellar I found the watchmans' hat and coat.
    C. The persons living in adjacent apartments stated that they had heard no unusual noises.
    D. Neither a knife or any firearms were found in the room.

12. The one of the following sentences which contains NO error in usage is:
    A. The policeman lay a firm hand on the suspect's shoulder.
    B. It is true that neither strength nor agility are the most important requirement for a good patrolman.
    C. Good citizens constantly strive to do more than merely comply the restraints imposed by society.
    D. Twenty years is considered a severe sentence for a felony.

13. Select the sentence containing an adverbial objective. 13.____
    A. Concepts can only acquire content when they are connected, however indirectly, with sensible experience.
    B. The cloth was several shades too light to match the skirt which she had discarded.
    C. The Gargantuan Hall of Commons became a tri-daily horror to Kurt, because two youths discerned that he had a beard and courageously told the world about it.
    D. Brooding morbidly over the event, Elsie found herself incapable of engaging in normal activity.

14. Select the sentence containing a verb in the subjunctive mood. 14.____
    A. Had he known of the new experiments with penicillin dust for the cure of colds, he might have been tempted to try them in his own office.
    B. I should be very much honored by your visit.
    C. Though he has one of the highest intelligence quotients in his group, he seems far below the average in actual achievement.
    D. Long had I known that he would be the man finally selected for such signal honors.

15. Select the sentence containing one (or more) passive perfect participle(s). 15.____
    A. Having been apprised of the consequences of his refusal to answer, the witness finally revealed the source of his information.
    B. To have been placed in such an uncomfortable position was perhaps unfair to a journalist of his reputation.
    C. When deprived of special immunity he had, of course, no alternative but to speak.
    D. Having been obdurate until now, he was reluctant to surrender under this final pressure exerted upon him.

16. Select the sentence containing a predicate nominative. 16.____
    A. His dying wish, which he expressed almost with his last breath, was to see that justice was done toward his estranged wife.
    B. So long as we continue to elect our officials in truly democratic fashion, we shall have the power to preserve our liberties.
    C. We could do nothing, at this juncture, but walk the five miles back to camp.
    D. There was the spaniel, wet and cold and miserable, waiting silently at the door.

17. Select the sentence containing exactly TWO adverbs. 17.____
    A. The gentlemen advanced with exasperating deliberateness, while his lonely partner waited.
    B. If you are well, will you come early?
    C. I think you have guessed right, though you were rather slow, I must say.
    D. The last hundred years have seen more change than a thousand years of the Roman Empire, than a hundred thousand years of the stone age.

Questions 18-24.

DIRECTIONS: Select the choice describing the error in the sentence.

18. If us seniors do not support school functions, who will?
    A. Unnecessary shift in tense
    B. Incomplete sentence
    C. Improper case of pronoun
    D. Lack of parallelism

19. The principal has issued regulations which, in my opinion, I think are too harsh.
    A. Incorrect punctuation
    B. Faulty sentence structure
    C. Misspelling
    D. Redundant expression

20. The freshmens' and sophomores' performances equaled those of the juniors and seniors.
    A. Ambiguous reference
    B. Incorrect placement of punctuation
    C. Misspelling of past tense
    D. Incomplete comparison

21. Each of them, Anne and her, is an outstanding pianist I can't tell you which one is best.
    A. Lack of agreement
    B. Improper degree of comparison
    C. Incorrect case of pronoun
    D. Run-on sentence

22. She wears clothes that are more expensive than my other friends.
    A. Misuse of *than*
    B. Incorrect relative pronoun
    C. Shift in tense
    D. Faulty comparison

23. At the very end of the story it implies that the children's father died tragically.
    A. Misuse of *implies*
    B. Indefinite use of pronoun
    C. Incorrect spelling
    D. Incorrect possessive

24. At the end of the game both of us, John and me, couldn't scarcely walk because we were so tired.
    A. Incorrect punctuation
    B. Run-on sentence
    C. Incorrect case of pronoun
    D. Double negative

Questions 25-30.

DIRECTIONS: Questions 25 through 30 consist of a sentence lacking certain needed punctuation. Pick as your answer the description of punctuation which will CORRECTLY complete the sentence.

25. If you take the time to keep up your daily correspondence you will no doubt be most efficient.
    A. Comma only after *doubt*
    B. Comma only after *correspondence*
    C. Commas after *correspondence*, *will*, and *be*
    D. Commas after *if*, *correspondence*, and *will*

26. Because he did not send the application soon enough he did not receive the   26.____
    up to date copy of the book.
    A. Commas after *application* and *enough,* and quotation marks before *up* and after *date*
    B. Commas after *application* and *enough,* and hyphens between *to* and *date*
    C. Comma after *enough,* and hyphens between *up* and *to* and between *to* and *date*
    D. Comma after *application,* and quotation marks before *up* and after *date*

27. The coordinator requested from the department the following items a letter each   27.____
    week summarizing progress personal forms and completed applications for tests.
    A. Commas after *items* and *completed*
    B. Semi-colon after *items* and *progress,* comma after *forms*
    C. Colon after *items,* commas after *progress* and *forms*
    D. Colon after *items,* commas after *forms* and *applications*

28. The supervisor asked Who will attend the conference next month.   28.____
    A. Comma after *asked,* period after *month*
    B. Period after *asked,* question mark after *month*
    C. Comma after *asked,* quotation marks before *Who,* quotation marks after *month,* and question mark after the quotation marks
    D. Comma after *asked,* quotation marks before *Who,* question mark after *month,* and quotation marks after the question mark

29. When the statistics are collected, we will forward the results to you as soon as   29.____
    possible.
    A. Comma after *you*
    B. Commas after *forward* and *you*
    C. Commas after *collected, results* and *you*
    D. Comma after *collected*

30. The ecology of our environment is concerned with mans pollution of the   30.____
    atmosphere.
    A. Comma after *ecology*
    B. Apostrophe after *n* and before *s* in *mans*
    C. Commas after *ecology* and *environment*
    D. Apostrophe after *s* in *mans*

KEY (CORRECT ANSWERS)

1.	D	11.	C	21.	B
2.	A	12.	D	22.	D
3.	D	13.	B	23.	B
4.	A	14.	A	24.	D
5.	B	15.	A	25.	B
6.	D	16.	A	26.	C
7.	A	17.	C	27.	C
8.	C	18.	C	28.	D
9.	A	19.	D	29.	D
10.	A	20.	B	30.	B

TEST 3

DIRECTIONS: Each question or incomplete statement is followed by several suggested answers or completions. Select the one that BEST answers the question or completes the statement. *PRINT THE LETTER OF THE CORRECT ANSWER IN THE SPACE AT THE RIGHT.*

Questions 1-6.

DIRECTIONS: From the four choices offered in Questions 1 through 6, select the one which is INCORRECT.

1. A. Before we try to extricate ourselves from this struggle in which we are now engaged in, we must be sure that we are not severing ties of honor and duty.
    B. Besides being an outstanding student, he is also a leader in school government and a trophy-winner in school sports.
    C. If the framers of the Constitution were to return to life for a day, their opinion of our amendments would be interesting.
    D. Since there are three m's in the word, it is frequently misspelled.

    1.____

2. A. It was a college with an excellance beyond question.
    B. The coach will accompany the winners, whomever they may be.
    C. The dean, together with some other faculty members, is planning a conference.
    D. The jury are arguing among themselves.

    2.____

3. A. This box is less nearly square than that one.
    B. Wagner is many persons' choice as the world's greatest composer.
    C. The habits of Copperheads are different from Diamond Backs.
    D. The teacher maintains that the child was insolent.

    3.____

4. A. There was a time when the Far North was unknown territory. Now American soldiers manning radar stations there wave to Boeing jet planes zooming by overhead.
    B. Exodus, the psalms, and Deuteronomy are all books of the Old Testament.
    C. Linda identified her china dishes by marking their bottoms with india ink.
    D. Harry S. Truman, former president of the United States, served as a captain in the American army during World War I.

    4.____

5. A. The sequel of their marriage was a divorce.
    B. We bought our car secondhand.
    C. His whereabouts is unknown.
    D. Jones offered to use his own car, providing the company would pay for gasoline, oil, and repairs,

    5.____

6. A. I read Golding's "Lord of the Flies".
   B. The orator at the civil rights rally thrilled the audience when he said, "I quote Robert Burns's line, 'A man's a man for a' that."
   C. The phrase "producer to consumer" is commonly used by market analysts.
   D. The lawyer shouted, "Is not this evidence illegal?"

6._____

Questions 7-9.

DIRECTIONS: In answering Questions 7 through 9, mark the letter A if faulty because of incorrect grammar, mark the letter B if faulty because of incorrect punctuation, mark the letter C if correct.

7. Mr. Brown our accountant, will audit the accounts next week.

7._____

8. Give the assignment to whomever is able to do it most efficiently.

8._____

9. The supervisor expected either your or I to file these reports.

9._____

Questions 10-14.

DIRECTIONS: In each of the following groups of four sentences, one sentence contains an error in sentence structure, grammar, usage, diction, or punctuation. Indicate the INCORRECT sentence.

10. A. The agent asked, "Did you say, 'Never again?'"
    B. Kindly let me know whether you can visit us on the 17th.
    C. "I cannot accept that!" he exploded. "Please show me something else.
    D. Ed, will you please lend me your grass shears for an hour or so.

10._____

11. A. Recalcitrant though he may have been, Alexander was willfully destructive.
    B. Everybody should look out for himself.
    C. John is one of those students who usually spends most of his time in the principal's office.
    D. She seems to feel that what is theirs is hers.

11._____

12. A. Be he ever so much in the wrong, I'll support the man while deploring his actions.
    B. The schools' lack of interest in consumer education is shortsighted.
    C. I think that Fitzgerald's finest stanza is one which includes the reference to youth's "sweet-scented manuscript.
    D. I never would agree to Anderson having full control of the company's policies.

12._____

13. A. We had to walk about five miles before finding a gas station.
    B. The willful sending of a false alarm has, and may, result in homicide.
    C. Please bring that book to me at once.
    D. Neither my sister nor I am interested in bowling.

13._____

14. A. He is one of the very few football players who doesn't wear a helmet with a face guard.
    B. But three volunteers appeared at the recruiting office.
    C. Such consideration as you can give us will be appreciated.
    D. When I left them, the group were disagreeing about the proposed legislation.

Question 15.

DIRECTIONS: Question 15 contains two sentences concerning criminal law. The sentences could contain errors in English grammar or usage. A sentence does not contain an error simply because it could be written in a different manner. In answering this question, choose answer
- A. if only sentence I is correct
- B. if only sentence II is correct
- C. if both sentences are correct
- D. if neither sentence is correct

15. I. The use of fire or explosives to destroy tangible property is proscribed by the criminal mischief provisions of the Revised Penal Law.
    II. The defendant's taking of a taxicab for the immediate purpose of affecting his escape did not constitute grand larceny.

KEY (CORRECT ANSWERS)

1.	A	6.	A	11.	C
2.	B	7.	B	12.	D
3.	C	8.	A	13.	B
4.	B	9.	A	14.	A
5.	D	10	A	15.	A

www.ingramcontent.com/pod-product-compliance
Lightning Source LLC
Chambersburg PA
CBHW082039300426
44117CB00015B/2534